When I think of Bill Cole, INTEGRITY is the first word that jumps to my lips. Bill is truly one of the most amazing and knowledgeable business professionals with whom I've had the pleasure of working. In the focused time I've been privileged to share with Bill, I have learned how to better evaluate my own processes, how to increase my productivity, thereby improving my output and bottom line. My business continues to grow as a direct result of what I've learned from Bill Cole and I cannot think of anyone more deserving of my recommendation.

Arminda Lindsay, Vice President,
Whetstone Leadership, Greensboro, North Carolina

Bill is a clear-thinking leader with passion, vision, and an amazing ability to communicate. He is equally effective in one-on-one counseling sessions and enthralling hundreds in a training session.

Dan Panzica, Sr. VP Operations, Chief Quality Officer
Source Photonics, Chengdu, China

Working with Bill Cole and ABS has afforded the staff at Meyer US the opportunity to grow and expand the leadership capabilities of our senior management team. Through regular professional sessions facilitated by Bill, our leadership team has developed into a cohesive and motivated group and have translated our training into accelerated performance of our individual teams and the company.

Jenny Bledsoe, VP HR & Consumer Relations
Meyer U.S. Corp., Vallejo, California

Thank you for the great service you deliver. Every one of the 10 employees attending has given the program high marks.

David Rex Moore, President
Rex Moore Group, Inc., Sacramento, California

Thank you for helping me to be a better person and a leader.

Pam Knoblock, Human Resources Manager
Systems 3, Inc., Sacramento, California

This man is a master facilitator, instructor, writer, coach, businessperson, and sage. It was chance that allowed working with Bill as I was examining a business opportunity about a decade ago. He was a terrific example and mentor. I did move forward with the business opportunity and had the opportunity to work with him for many years. He is a professional in every way. The way he demonstrates this is to his customers by helping them become more productive and profitable without any compromise. I care deeply about this man and his exceptional work. You will too!

Jim Ullery, President,
Center for Organizational Energy, Ft. Myers, Florida

Having worked for a Fortune 10 company, Bill is one of the best trainers I've ever seen.

Joanne Warren, Director of Human Resources
Level One Communications, Sacramento, California

With profound and heartfelt appreciation, the Impact Photographics' Team would like to thank you for your dedication, commitment, effort, desire, passion, enthusiasm, attitude, and ability to make a difference in our lives and in the lives of so many others.

Jeff Wagner, VP/General Manager
Impact Photo-graphics. El Dorado Hills, California

Every business owner, indeed every business person, would be fortunate to have Bill Cole on their speed dial and in their quiver!

Doug Lindley, Owner
First Service Insurance, Roseville, California

Bill Cole gets it! So much so that after just one day of his training, I was able to better educate, motivate, and 'loyaltate' an existing customer ready to defect. To date, they've been one of my best revenue-generating customers. Thank you, Bill.

Jeff Peterson, President
Business Performance Solutions, Inc., Atlanta, Georgia

Thank you for being such a terrific mentor to me and hundreds of other people. You really have been an important part of my development as a business person, and I appreciate it.

Dr. Tom Anderson, President
Visitube, Inc., Sacramento, California
Founder, Berkeley Antibody Co., Berkeley, California

Bill Cole's work with many of my business clients has proven to be both profitable for them and enlightening. Bill is a real pro, coach and confidant. He will enhance your business and provide systems to keep your outcomes on track.

John B. Kelly, CFP, Author; Speaker, Life Coach
The Investor's Caddie, Inc., Sacramento, California

Bill Cole is a wonderful facilitator. He combines high energy with a commitment to training; it is a winning combination. Bill has a way of encouraging participation from everyone and making sessions meaningful and fun.

Betti Spencer, Training and Development Coordinator
Placer Savings Bank, Auburn, California

Bill Cole has been very responsive to our specific needs and has followed up on the progress of the course participants regularly. Feedback from students has been very positive and their level of commitment extremely high. Associates view selection for this course as a great recommendation from higher management and the class is taken very seriously here at DST Output.

Scott Shelton, Sr. Vice President, Operations
DST Output Technology, El Dorado Hills, California

"Bill Cole is an effective coach, trainer and facilitator because of his real knowledge of the challenges facing today's business leaders. He helps business leaders put theory into effective and positive practice."

Nancy Faunce, President and CEO
FasTracKids International, Ltd., Denver, Colorado

There are many good business people in the world. There are equally as many great trainers in the world. Rarely do you get the best of both worlds together. Bill Cole is that guy. He not only knows business, but is adept at the business of teaching business principles that businesses need. My exposure to Bill Cole has been one of the best booster shots to my business career.

Mark Giganti, Training Director
Crestcom International, LLC, Denver, Colorado

Bill Cole is epitome of living a congruent life in terms of values and daily action driven by a clear mission. With profound ethics, he is devoted to developing the potential of human talent. Bill approaches his work with the same energy, enthusiasm, and professionalism whether it's as a master facilitator, a communicator, or as an educator in everything he does. The best gift we can receive from Bill – besides his friendship – is this book, replete with wisdom for current and future generations.

Gerardo Hurtado, Managing Director
Management Int. de Mexico, Monterrey, Mexico

When you combine the words Passion - Dedication - Patience - Intensity - and Results, this can only add up to mean Bill Cole. Having worked with Bill for over 15 years, he has shown an incredible consistency and desire to help others succeed - even at his own personal expense. I have leaned on Bill for a myriad of situations and he has always come through with a perspective that I hadn't considered. He has a keen knack for being able to "see around the corner" and then predict what's around the "next corner". He is an invaluable and critical asset to anyone looking to raise their level of performance.

Tim Parenti, President
MVP Dynamics, Chicago, Illionois

Thanks again for how much you have helped my career.
David Green, President/CEO
Contra Costa Federal Credit Union, Martinez, California

It is a genuine honor for me that Bill Cole has become a trusted ally, mentor, and dear friend. He continues to play a pivotal role in my leadership development and has proven to be a valuable source of information and support. Bill Cole will facilitate your leadership development and growth in a time when relationships are the foundation for success. I can say with all sincerity Bill will inspire you to become immeasurably more than what you believed possible.

Cheryl Rogers, Controller
Intech Mechanical, Roseville, California

Thank you for delivering a speech that changed my life.

Cynthia Meyers, CFP, Sacramento, California

I found you to be the most amazing facilitator I've ever had at any training.

Lynn Quijada-Splan, Director of Business Development
Warden's Office Products, Modesto, California

Thank you for sharing all that you have and making the class fun! I truly admire your capabilities in leadership and I believe as the old saying goes: "You walk the talk."

Kimberly Manning, Finance & Admin. Manager
The Warden's Office Inc., Modesto, California

Bill is a Fantastic Trainer and Facilitator! His communication skills and program content are among the best I have ever heard. Bill is a 10+ every single program.

Jim Pelley, CSP, Founder, Laughter Works
President & CEO, uLinkNetwork, Folsom, California

"I wanted you to know that the classes and seminars you provided for us in Fresno were an important element in the success we had for a few years. We were the top market in the US for two years."

Jerry Meyerson, Director of Operations
McDonald's Corporation

Having been in the training industry for over 30 years and working with some of the best including Zig Ziglar for 7 years, I have seen a lot of true professionals. Bill Cole is one of those true professionals. Even though I have conducted over 2000 seminars myself, when I hear and see Bill on the platform I always learn something new. He exemplifies what a true professional really is in the training industry, but more importantly over the 15 years I have known him he has become a real friend. Thanks Bill for all your help and best of luck for the future.

David Curry, President
Professional Presentations, Inc., Dallas, Texas

Three years ago I met Bill Cole. At the time, Meyer Corp. U.S. was experiencing tremendous growth. We also recognized that communication and collaboration inside our company was in need of vast improvement if we were to maintain future momentum. When I introduced Bill Cole to our executive team I said he was a world class facilitator. Today, I believe that just as strongly. Our executive and management teams have gone through a major positive transformation as a result of our work together. I am also happy to report that Meyer has identified new strengths and continues to build healthy growth.

Jay Zilinskas, Managing Director
Meyer U.S., Vallejo, California

I have known Bill for more than 15 years working with him in the training industry. He is creative, ethical and one of the best curriculum developers and trainers I have ever known. When Bill says he is going to do something he does it with great vigor, thoughtfulness and discipline. When Bill has something to say it is worth listening to.

Bob Weber, President
Webcorp Development, Phoenix, Arizona

THE ABC FORMULA
Building Your Life's Enduring Core Values

This Book's Purpose is to inspire others
to establish enduring Core Values to
guide the journeys of their lives.

WM E Cole

William E. Cole

Authority Publishing
Gold River, California

The ABC Formula: Building Your Life's Enduring Core Values

By William E. Cole

1. Self-Help : Personal Growth - Success 2. Business & Economics : Leadership 3. Family & Relationships : Ethics & Morals

ISBN: 978-1-935953-26-5

Cover Design and Graphics by Katherine Tippin
katherinetippin@gmail.com

Printed in the United States of America

Authority Publishing

11230 Gold Express Dr. #310-413
Gold River, CA 95670
800-877-1097

www.AuthorityPublishing.com

Contents

Preface

This book pays tribute to special individuals who positively impacted my life. I sincerely hope to inspire others to follow their chosen path in a more meaningful way and with a greater depth of purpose. As you prepare to read *The ABC Formula*, be aware of two underlying premises intended to help you get the most out of reading this book.

First, I serve business owners, entrepreneurs, executives, and other organizational leaders whom I hold in high regard. Therefore, I always capitalize the word Client. My intent is to honor them and not distract you.

Second, I recommend you read the book in sequence. While it is entirely possible to benefit from reading first the chapters that intrigue you most, the Core Values progress from one to the next, each building on the other. You will get the most out of this book by reading it in order. I encourage you to do just that.

Bill Cole, Founder, President, and CEO

PART ONE
PROLOGUE

Dedication

How Desperation
Turned into Inspiration

The ABC Formula

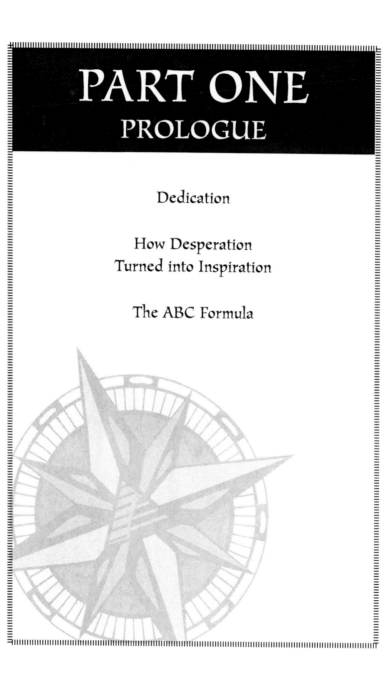

Dedication

This book covers many life lessons that shaped me and others. While I specialize in helping others become more effective leaders, *The ABC Formula* is relevant for you regardless of the particular path you chose – or are in process of choosing.

As indicated by the first chapter's title, *How Desperation Turned into Inspiration*, this book starts off with a painful experience. I admit it's an unusual way to start an inspirational book. But it sets up an important lesson. Regardless of the circumstances you find yourself in at any moment in time, possibilities exist, and growth occurs if approached correctly. Out of tragedy often comes triumph. We all benefit from that knowledge.

This book is first dedicated to Norm on his seventy-third birthday. His mentorship has had a deep and most profound impact on my life. In addition, I've been blessed by other role models who deeply touched my life. For them, my appreciation grows even more as the days fly by. I sincerely hope you will get to know and learn from them as you read this.

As a by-product, you will also get to know me better. In spite of my shortcomings, weaknesses, and setbacks, my role models led me to discover opportunities for growth and accomplishment I never would have imagined without them. Although it would take an entire book to acknowledge all the mentors, colleagues, friends, affiliates, and Clients who have positively impacted my life, acknowledgements are in order for five special people.

First is my wife, Kristy. I cherish her, for she is the love of my life. We have built a great life together. She is my business partner, confidant, and the most wonderful supporter a spouse could ever experience.

Second is Benton Minor. As a college professor and mentor, he touched my life in significant ways. Without his intercession and guidance, I would have accomplished much less.

Third is Dr. Paul Eickmann. As a college professor, administrator, mentor, and friend, his influence changed the trajectory of my career. At a critical turning point in my life, his impact opened new vistas for me in ways that continue to this day. Thank you, Paul, for the knowledge, guidance, and opportunities you gave me. My debt to you is deep indeed.

Fourth is Dr. Chris Alford. His feedback on this book helped shape my approach. And most importantly, he deeply impacted my life in many ways during the past few years. We've shared much together. Chris, I treasure our friendship.

Fifth is Dr. Ellen Koehler. Ellen participated in two of my leadership development courses, including the one where I first publicly shared the story you will read in chapter one. As my primary reader and friend, her thoughtful feedback, patience, and insightful collegial guidance were invaluable and instrumental to complete this work. Ellen, I owe you a most heartfelt thank you. Know that I deeply appreciate you and am blessed by our friendship.

In addition, you will read stories about, find references to, and contemplate quotations from many others who have inspired me. They include presidents, business leaders, authors, songwriters, athletes, coaches, philosophers, religious leaders, military heroes, and professional speakers. Let me also draw special attention to Dr. Anonymous, my favorite philosopher. Throughout history, wise sages dispensed advice that has sometimes gone unattributed to its originator. This is my humorous attempt to pay homage to them.

May this book serve and inspire you. Let's begin the journey.

How Desperation Turned into Inspiration

February 9th is a day I'll never forget. The howling wind lashed the window of the corner office on this cool, dreary, and overcast afternoon when suddenly, the phone rang. My wife, Kristy, asked for me to be interrupted. I thought, "How unusual. She knows never to interrupt me in a Client meeting – particularly these bank executives." But she insisted it was really important.

As I impatiently held the phone to my ear I heard, "Norm and Kathy have been in a car accident." I don't remember much else about the conversation. I only knew I needed to get on a plane. My heart was pounding, and my mind was racing.

A classic self-made entrepreneur, Norm recruited me to join the company at its beginning. His track record of building four successful companies attracted me initially. But Norm and his wife, Kathy, weren't ready for early retirement. They already tried it – twice before.

In the previous eight and a half years, Norm became my mentor and one of my best friends. He became the older, wiser brother I never had growing up. Things were going well for us in the business. The previous calendar year was the company's best ever. In the previous month, we broke all sales records.

As we grew the company, Norm challenged me and another staff member, Ron, with seemingly impossible tasks and deadlines. Norm had vision, charisma, and a strong sense of obligation. His leadership was usually right on target. He led us to drive ourselves to accomplish our goals. As a result, we had already helped more than 3,000

Clients achieve their goals.

After hanging up the phone, I spent the next two hours rushing around postponing meetings and commitments, and reserved a late afternoon flight. Ron and his wife, Karrie, plus Norm's daughter, Laura, met me at the airport. They'd been in touch with the doctor and filled me in on what little details were known. Norm's injuries were substantial. He faced a lengthy recuperation period. We were all sure he wouldn't like that. Norm was a man of action. We grabbed a quick bite of nondescript food from the airport cafeteria. Meaningful conversation was futile. Our thoughts were far away.

As we waited, impatiently fidgeting, time seemed to stand still. Our flight was delayed. We were anxious to get there. Minutes dragged into hours. Finally, we took off. By the time we arrived at the hospital, it was about 10 p.m. The doctor met us in the lobby and hurried us into a waiting room. In detail, he described what happened.

The accident was a bad one. It was on a mountain pass. Everyone was driving carefully and traveling slowly, but no one saw the patch of black ice. Norm and Kathy's Bronco lost traction and started sliding – head on into an oncoming 18-wheeler. The front end of the Bronco was crushed by the truck, and the steering wheel slammed directly into Norm's chest. The seat belt tightened around Kathy's upper body, separating all her ribs and fracturing a vertebrae in her back. As the big truck pushed the Bronco backwards, it spun 180 degrees and slammed into the side of the mountain. When the paramedics arrived at the scene, they used the "jaws of life" to extract them from the crushed vehicle.

Rushed to a local hospital, Kathy was having difficulty breathing but stable. Norm's injuries were too severe to be treated by anyone less than a top heart specialist. That meant an airlift. As the paramedics loaded him on the helicopter, something burst in his chest. They performed an emergency procedure on the spot to stabilize his heart. They saved his life right there. Then he was airlifted to the hospital. He was conscious and aware as they wheeled him into the operating room. The doctors worked diligently on Norm to stabilize him. But then suddenly, something went wrong.

The doctor said he was sorry. When Norm's aorta burst, they lost him. He died just as we arrived at the hospital. We didn't even get to say goodbye. As I glanced around the room, everyone was in a state of shock. Ron looked numb, which was how we all felt. Norm was a hero to all of us. No one was sure what to say or do. I thought, "How could anyone know what to do in this situation? Ron and Laura just lost their dad." And I wasn't much better. Norm was not only my business associate, my mentor, and my friend, he was also my brother.

Later, as I stared at Norm's lifeless body to pay my final respects, I asked myself, "Why does it take losing someone to pay attention to the teacher?" My head pounded and my chest heaved through the wrenching sobs as I searched for an answer to that difficult question. I was hurting on the inside. My stomach was tied up in knots, and my breathing was shallow.

Afterwards I checked into a hotel at the airport. I don't even remember its name. In that sterile room, I fell on my knees, crying and heartbroken. As Abraham Lincoln once said, "I have been driven many times upon my knees by the overwhelming conviction that I had nowhere else to go. My own wisdom, and that of all about me, seemed insufficient for the day."[1] That's exactly how I felt. I knew I couldn't go on alone. I needed to submit and ask for help. I prayed for guidance to give me strength and courage to go on. I asked for understanding: "God, why did this happen? Why did you take Norm away from us?" I prayed for wisdom and revelation: "What do you want from me? What do you want me to do?" When I got off my knees and into bed, I tossed and turned the bedcovers restlessly and continuously during that most distressing and difficult night of my life.

When we lose someone we care deeply about, the questions reach into the depths of our souls. The floodgate couldn't be turned off, as the questions ran through my mind. There were so many. And they concerned more than just work and business. Norm's lessons transcended work. I kept asking, "What had I learned from Norm? What were the gems and the pearls of wisdom?"

Honestly, we'd never been close as kids. While he was my sibling, he was ten years older. Working together closely during these eight and a half years had given me new insight. Norm touched my life deeply. He had the unique ability to reach out and touch people's lives. Everyone who knew him was a better person because of it.

Norm often said, "Aren't we all about having a positive impact on other people's lives? After all, working with Clients on their business challenges is just a vehicle for impacting their lives. We're in the helping business. Sometimes, our help will result in saving lives." That began to make sense and gave me a focus. I gained enough clarity and direction to get some sleep.

When I awoke, I rededicated myself to that vision and rewrote my personal mission statement: "To positively impact people's lives." I re-focused and committed to a new measure of success with this daily question: "How well did I positively impact people's lives today?" That's what drives me.

And there were many other important lessons. Norm often said, "It's not so much the destination as the direction and the journey. Don't just focus on the goals. They're important, but not just for the end result. They're important for setting you on the path. What's more important is who you are and how you get there. It's about your character."

As that sank in, I realized people were attracted to Norm because of his character. I remembered him tell me, "Most people say that adversity builds character, but I disagree. Adversity *tests* character." I asked myself, "Was I now being tested? If this *is* a test, then what defined Norm's character?"

I thought deeply about our company, Advanced Business Concepts, Inc. In a nutshell, we taught business owners the ABCs of business. But it was more than that. I asked myself, "What was the essence of what we *really* did?"

In a blinding flash of inspiration, I understood with great clarity what ABC meant. It was as if Norm spoke directly to me at that precise moment. ABC means to have the right attitude, belief, and conviction about what you do. I smiled as I fondly remembered one specific instance, when Norm told me that I was certainly smart enough to be successful. But he added that being smart isn't enough, as he pointed his finger to the side of his head and shook it sideways. He said, "It's more about who you are on the inside," and pointed his finger directly at my heart.

As I recall that precise moment, I now realize how much *The ABC Formula* is at the heart of what has built my character. *The ABC Formula* is the source of passion for what we do. Passion is the energy of the soul. Passion gives you energy, which creates your power. What burns on the inside shines on the outside. Passion fuels your mission.

With *The ABC Formula*, you walk your talk. You're a role model for everyone around you. Your attitude, belief, and conviction define your life's enduring Core Values. They are deeply ingrained. You would never, *ever* compromise them.

We could always count on Norm to do the right thing. He

always acted based on his Core Values. Suddenly I realized, *"That's* what made Norm... *Norm."* It was his enduring Core Values, the things he stood for – no matter what. His Core Values gave him charisma. They defined his character. They fueled his passion and purpose. That's why people were attracted to him.

So I asked myself, "What Core Values did Norm hold dear? What did he strive for every day of his life? What were those important lessons? What are the Core Values I will strive for every day for the rest of my life?"

Suddenly, just as if Norm again spoke directly to me, inspiring phrases rushed into my mind. In just a few seconds, I wrote the following:

Core Values of Norman H. Cole (1938-1994)
Founder, Advanced Business Concepts, Inc.

1. *Be Respectful of Everyone You Come In Contact With.*
2. *Be in Control of Yourself and Maintain Your Integrity.*
3. *Be Willing to Serve Others and Be There for the Right Reason.*
4. *Be Totally Honest and Transparent.*
5. *Be Willing to Do the Work Necessary to Find Out the Truth.*
6. *Take the Initiative.*
7. *Be Accountable to Your Commitments.*

When I finished writing, I re-read them – ready to edit and ready to make them better. The longer I looked, the more I knew I couldn't change a word. I didn't care whether the grammar was correct or not. Those were Norm's attitudes, beliefs, and convictions summarized by these Core Values. They communicated exactly the right message. Finally, a sense of comfort enveloped me. An inner peace gave me the strength to face the day. With these Core Values guiding me, I knew I could face the challenges of an uncertain future without Norm's guidance as my mentor.

Then a new reality struck home. A sense of urgency overcame me to comfort my business associates, friends, family, and particularly, Mom. There's nothing more difficult for a parent than losing a child. I comprehended the biblical story of Abraham's willingness to sacrifice his son, Isaac, with more light and clarity than ever before.

When I arrived home later that morning, our top salesperson, Dave Schmitt, was waiting on my doorstep. Instinctively, he knew something was wrong. He took Norm's death hard. We cried together. To comfort him, I shared the Core Values I was inspired to write. He was deeply touched.

Later and without telling me, Dave asked a Client, Andy, to engrave those words on a clock. When Dave picked it up, Andy told him that customers and students from the local university saw it in his store. The power of the words touched them, and they asked for copies. This clock, Dave's thoughtful gift to me, now hangs in my office.

Several days later, I met with Ruby, a longtime Client. I shared Norm's Core Values with her. She was particularly struck by number four, "Be Totally Honest and Transparent." She asked permission to share it at a stewardship meeting in her church the following week. Ruby later told me that the power of the words and the story of losing Norm touched people and moved many to tears. Over the next few months, several Clients commented on the difference they noticed in me. They said I was a changed man.

That cold, dreary, and windy February day started me on a new journey. There are many unexpected curves in the highway of life. We rarely travel in a straight line. Core Values guide you as a beacon of light shining through the darkness surrounding you. Core Values give you the framework to touch lives positively as you walk on your path. Core Values help you stay focused and become more purposeful. Core Values show you how and when to move in a specific direction. Core Values define you. They are

The ABC Formula at work in you. The right attitude, belief, and conviction about who you are and what you do gives you congruence as to *how* you travel on your road. *The ABC Formula* is a key foundation for your life.

Today, I'm the Founder, President, and CEO of Advanced Business Solutions, Inc. I'm an author, speaker, trainer, executive coach, facilitator, and consultant. In my career, I am privileged to have worked with and touched the lives of several thousand people.

Whenever I share Norm's Core Values, they inspire and touch people's lives. His enduring Core Values positively impact people's lives. In fifty-five years, Norm fully developed and lived these Core Values before he was taken from us in his prime. They defined a large part of his character. Now they are a meaningful part of Norm's legacy. They are his gift to me and to you. They are incredible life lessons.

In our darkest and most challenging moments, it is possible to find the emotional courage to become what we have always been capable of becoming. It's all about our attitude, belief, and conviction. *The ABC Formula* fuels your purpose and passion, and drives your mission.

I'm now older than Norm was when he died. When I started building my life's enduring Core Values, the process turned desperation into inspiration. Each and every day, I embrace this new level of awareness. As I continue my journey, I strive to consistently apply them in all I do.

It took losing someone I loved to bring these enduring Core Values to life. I wouldn't wish that painful experience on anyone. But the truth is — that's what inspired this book. May this now inspire you and positively impact your life.

Norman H. Cole (1938-1994)
Founder, President, and CEO
Advanced Business Concepts, Inc.

Chapter One Endnotes

1. Abraham Lincoln. Great-Quotes.com, Gledhill Enterprises, 2011. http://www.great-quotes.com/quote/902393, accessed January 12, 2011.

The ABC Formula

*What we need is education in the obvious
rather than investigation of the obscure.*[1]
Oliver Wendell Holmes, Jr.
U.S. Supreme Court Justice

D o you remember learning your ABCs in school, the building blocks of reading and writing? How well you applied those building blocks determined to a large degree how successfully you achieved good grades in school. In a similar way, we need to apply other building blocks in our lives, and for similar results. Apply them right now. School is in session. It's called life.

For these building blocks, the raw materials already exist in us. They provide the foundation for self-concept – the way we perceive who we are. These building blocks create *The ABC Formula* which, to a large extent, guides our future. The good news is this: our attitudes, beliefs, and convictions give us a great deal of power and control over our journey. Let's start with the first building block.

Attitude

Attitudes count more than achievements.[2]
Rick Warren, Author

Attitudes form the foundation of all personal and professional relationships. They determine how we approach tasks and studies. They positively – or negatively – impact all areas of our lives. What's interesting is the influence and control we have over our own attitudes. Renowned Harvard psychologist and philosopher William James said, "The greatest discovery of my generation is that a human being can alter his life by altering his attitude."[3]

That's an important concept. Do you believe that you can alter your life by changing your attitude? I do. In my work, I've found that there are two fundamental factors that motivate most of us: inspiration or fear. Unfortunately, fear drives many people. And what exactly is fear? One of the great professional speakers of all time, Zig Ziglar, defines fear as an acronym, "false evidence appearing real."[4]

This term applies not just to the fears we say out loud or the physical sense of certain dangers which compel us to take particular actions. At least as influential, if not more so, is the unspoken dialogue inside our heads. So here's an interesting question to consider. Which influences our self-concept more: our inner thoughts, the words we say to ourselves, or the ones we verbalize? Common estimates indicate people think as much as seven times faster than they speak. So the sheer volume of what goes on in our inner world of self-talk significantly influences our self-concept. To make matters worse, an estimated ninety percent of self-talk is negative. Ziglar gave this a memorable label: "Stinkin' Thinkin'."[5]

Another renowned professional speaker, Earl Nightingale, expanded on this concept. As a quick side note, my professional speaking career started a few days after Nightingale passed away. I dedicated my first speech to him. He revealed one of his most powerful concepts in his breakthrough work *The Strangest Secret.* In it, he described the subconscious mind in an easy-to-understand way. He said the subconscious mind is similar to an unplanted field. You can plant seeds and carefully fertilize and water them. Or you can plant weeds and do the same. The barren field cares not whether you plant seeds or weeds. Your efforts yield a bumper crop either way. So ask this question: what do I plant...seeds or weeds? As respected business author and syndicated columnist Harvey Mackay advises: "Don't water your weeds."[6]

Scientific evidence supports this line of thinking. Several research studies came to similar conclusions regarding the importance of attitude. A distinguished professor of psychology at University of North Carolina at Chapel Hill and author of the book *Positvity,* Dr. Barbara L. Fredrickson researched this topic extensively. Her research shows that a positive attitude makes a difference in personal well-being. When interviewed, she said, "Our emotions tend to obey a tipping point. My research shows that 'positivity ratio' is three to one. We need three positive emotions to lift us up for every one negative emotion that brings us down. Eighty percent of Americans only have a two to one positivity ratio."[7]

Scott Hunter, a Certified Speaking Professional and business coach, cites research sponsored by the Andrew Carnegie Foundation in the 1970s. In a study of more than 300,000 professionals, it concluded that 7 % of an individual's success was attributed to knowledge, 12% was attributed to skill, and 81% was determined by attitude.[8]

A study by Harvard University revealed that 85% of the reasons for success, accomplishments, promotions, etc. were because of our attitudes. Only 15% were because of our technical expertise.[9]

Another study conducted in the fall of 2002 by the professional services firm Towers Perrin studied 35,000 employees seeking to understand their feelings toward their jobs.[10] They also studied 100,100 employees from mid to large companies in North America. This second group described their feelings about their current work experience versus an ideal work experience.[11] A third group of 300 human resources professionals in the mid to large companies responded to similar questions. The combined data showed 55% of the workforce held negative feelings and 23% held positive feelings.

In 2008, the *Journal of Management* named Wayne F. Cascio as one of the most influential scholars in the field of management over the past 25 years. Cascio analyzed a study conducted by Gallup of 100,000 employees across 12 industries.[12] The study looked at the relationship between employee attitudes and business results including revenue, profits, customer loyalty, and employee retention. It concluded employee attitudes are critically important to the improvement of productivity. These research studies all reached similar conclusions. An individual's success is directly and overwhelmingly attributable to attitude. With this evidence, the first building block to work on right now is clear. Choose which attitudes you will embrace today. Attitude is a choice, and that choice is yours to make.[13]

And yet, the daily challenges we all face affect our ability to make the right choices. Unforeseen, unpredictable, and even unpleasant events and people drag us into unproductive attitudes in spite of our best intentions. When those inevitable challenges occur, we all need a reminder or a 'pick-me-up' to stay on track. I use this reinforcement. From respected author and teacher Charles Swindoll, it's the most powerful statement on attitude I know.

> The longer I live, the more I realize the impact of attitude on life. Attitude, to me, is more important than facts. It is more important than the past, than education, than money, than circumstances, than failures, than successes,

than what other people think or say or do. It is more important than appearance, giftedness or skill. It will make or break a company. It will cause a church to soar or sink. It will be the difference in a happy home or a home of horror. The remarkable thing is you have a choice every day regarding the attitude you will embrace for that day. We cannot change our past. We cannot change the fact that people will act in a certain way. We cannot change the inevitable. The only thing we can do is play on the one string we have, and that is our attitude.

I am convinced that life is 10 percent what happens to me and 90 percent how I react to it. And so it is with you.[14]

For me, the key point is this: it's not what happens *to* you, it's how you *deal* with what happens to you. Your attitude is ultimately your choice. A simple idea? Yes. Is it also powerful? Absolutely!

Some skeptics counter, "Isn't that just common sense?" Of course. It *is* common sense. However, this quote, attributed to the American cowboy philosopher of the twentieth century, Will Rogers, answers the skeptics who cross my path. He said, "Common sense ain't common."

Why is common sense uncommon? It's because common sense works best when we are rational. Unfortunately, in many situations when we allow our emotions take over, common sense takes a back seat along with our rational selves. Since fear drives so many people, and fear is *not* part of our rational side, it's no wonder that common sense isn't common. When we focus on the right attitude and look at things in positive ways, we learn another important building block. To a large degree, we control the attitudes we embrace. When we control our attitude and outlook, we determine – to a large degree – our outcomes.

January 15, 2009 provided a prime example of how this works under the most trying circumstances. Many of us were riveted to TV reports when US Airways Flight 1549 splashed down in spectacular fashion into the Hudson River. That plane was skillfully piloted by Captain Chelsey "Sully" Sullenberger. He and his crew were credited with saving 155 lives. 40 seconds after takeoff, both engines were knocked out by bird strikes. The jetliner glided without power above one of the most densely populated areas on earth, New York City. A tragedy loomed as a real possibility.

Captain Sully used every ounce of his 40 years of training and experience. He focused his attention on exactly what needed to be done. Given the circumstances, he responded with an extraordinarily positive attitude. This experienced US Airways pilot skillfully juggled the competing demands of keeping the wings perfectly even, keeping the rate of descent survivable and keeping the plane's nose slightly up – all without any power. As he talked on the radio with air traffic controllers, Sully maintained a serene tone. He later said this practiced tone came from years of experience. He knew this challenge needed to be faced squarely. There was a job to do. He never doubted he could pull off the water landing.

His confidence was also high in the crew's ability to evacuate the passengers once the plane landed. As the plane glided, the flight crew worked feverishly to keep the passengers focused on getting into the proper position to prepare for and absorb the crash. That was not an easy task. Many passengers peered out the windows at the looming frigid river or texted friends or family members as the plane was on its way down. The flight attendants started chanting, "Brace, brace, heads down, stay down." As the plane plummeted toward the Hudson, Captain Sully heard that chant over and over in the cockpit. It comforted and reassured him as his professional crew prepared for the next phase of the emergency landing.

At a later news conference, New York Mayor Michael Bloomberg commented on how masterfully Sully landed the plane in the river and made sure everyone got out safely. He noted that Sully walked the plane twice to verify if anyone was still onboard before he exited. The passengers scrambled outside and onto the plane's wings standing upright, as the river ferries and other boats converged to pick everyone up and take them to safety. It was quickly dubbed the *Miracle on the Hudson*.

15

An experienced and highly skilled pilot, Sully graduated from the U.S. Air Force Academy and received master's degrees from Purdue University and the University of Northern Colorado. No stranger to safety and accident investigations, he assisted in several National Transportation Safety Board probes. He served as safety chairman of the Air Line Pilots Association. He founded an air safety company, Safety Reliability Methods. Sully's skills in the cockpit that day had developed from years of training and experience.

Throughout his career, the attitudes of composure, focus, and self-control enabled him to maintain a positive outlook and rise to unexpected challenges. In a newscast interview, Sully's wife Lorraine commented about her husband's control and professionalism. James Ray, a spokesman for the U.S. Airline Pilots Association, characterized Sully as very calm, cool, relaxed, and professional. As Flight 1549 descended towards the Hudson River, Sully's attitude was every bit as important as his skills. He handled that emergency situation with flying colors.

Afterwards in a meeting between the crew and passengers, Sully greeted each passenger emotionally and warmly. He commented, "Holding up OK? Wild ride!" One passenger responded by quoting an old Irish saying: 'May the wind always be at your back and may God hold you safely in his hands.'

Captain Chelsey "Sully" Sullenberger deserves the credit, accolades, and acclaim he received. I believe he'd also say he just did what he trained all his life to do. He's an inspiring example of how to handle a situation – not only with great skill – but also with an outstanding attitude.

While most of us will never face a challenge of that magnitude, we all have the choice of which attitudes we embrace when we face challenges. How well we make those choices significantly impacts our lives. Each and every day, we can choose to approach life, situations, and people with positive attitudes and intentions. Or we can choose to be negative and fear or suspect the worst from people, situations, and life.

Fears drive people who make negative choices. Fears freeze them with inaction. Or they create excuses to stay in the present and maintain the status quo – no matter how painful it may be. Hope drives people who make positive choices. I choose this path. Which path, driven by which attitude, do you choose? Ultimately, this choice significantly influences your outlook and outcomes.

A dear friend is Dave Curry, one of the top sales professionals I've ever met. Dave was Zig Ziglar's top salesperson for many years. One of his most treasured possessions is a diamond-studded, gold-encrusted ring given to him by Zig who lovingly referred to him as a 'diamond in the rough.' His close friends know him as 'Diamond Dave.' When Dave owned a small business, he interviewed prospective employees with a key question. He asked each interviewee, "Are you a happy person?" It amazed him how much he learned from that simple and profound question. How would you answer?

The choice of happiness is a crucial one. Today, I encourage you to make a simple resolution. Be pleasant as you begin your day. When you start your day with a concerted effort to be happy and display a positive attitude, it significantly influences how your day unfolds. Early twentieth-century writer Elbert Hubbard promoted the concept to use intelligence to rid oneself of fear and bring health and happiness through service to others. He said, "Be pleasant until 10 o'clock in the morning and the rest of the day will take care of itself."[16] That's good advice. Will it work, each and every moment of each and every day? No. But when you sense yourself faltering, as I sometimes do, reinforce this building block with a simple quote from my favorite philosopher, Dr. Anonymous: "Any fact facing us is not as important as our attitude toward it, for that determines our success or failure."

Belief

*The outer conditions of a person's life will always be
found to reflect their inner beliefs.*[17]
James Lane Allen, Author

The second building block of *The ABC Formula* is belief.
Attitudes form our beliefs. One of the greatest scientists of
the twentieth century, Albert Einstein, made a surprising
statement about beliefs. He said the most fundamental
question we can ever ask ourselves is whether or not we
believe the universe we live in is friendly or hostile. He
hypothesized that our answer to that question determines
our destiny.

What precisely *do* you believe? Are people inherently good
and want to help you, or are they inherently bad and out to
get you? Do you believe life's challenges move you along a
path for growth... or destruction? People who believe the
world is out to get them often find it's true. Those who look
for the worst in people and believe they are inherently bad,
often find it in them. And worse, they attract those with
similar attitudes and beliefs.

The opposite is also true. When you look for the best in
people and believe they are inherently good, you see those
positive qualities and attract others with similar attitudes
and beliefs. These building blocks begin with positive
intention. They influence mightily your perceptions of the
world.

When we consistently approach situations and people
with particular attitudes, we condition our patterns of
thinking. As we consistently apply those thought patterns,
our attitudes form into beliefs. It starts with how we think.
Ralph Waldo Emerson, a philosopher, lecturer, essayist,

and poet was nicknamed the "Concord Sage." A leading voice for intellectual culture in nineteenth-century America, Emerson said, "We become what we think about all day long."[18]

What we think about entwines with what we believe. What do you think about all day long? What *do* you believe? Be honest with yourself. Is your thinking driven by inspiration and hope or fanned by the flames of fear? The great American industrialist and founder of the Ford Motor Company, Henry Ford, stated an ironic truth when he said, "Thinking is the hardest work there is... which is the probable reason why so few people engage in it."[19]

Thinking requires concentration. It can be hard work. But it also requires openness to new ideas. Frank Zappa, the rock musician and composer, is credited with saying, "The mind is like a parachute. It only works when it's open." How true!

With closed minds, we constrict ourselves to the rigidity of our comfort zone – no matter how uncomfortable it may be. When we condition our thinking to be open to new possibilities and points of view, we increase our degree of creativity and flexibility. With open minds, exciting possibilities emerge. Again, it's our choice to be open or closed-minded. We make this choice daily... or even more often.

History provides us with an example of how this works. In World War II, the Allied Armed Forces created a complex strategic and logistical plan to invade and liberate the European continent from Nazi control. As Supreme Allied Commander, General Dwight D. Eisenhower assembled a team of brilliant strategists including British General Bernard Montgomery, U.S. General Omar Bradley, and others. They assembled the largest naval armada in history. They planned and rehearsed the massive D-Day invasion in the greatest possible detail. The invasion troops included the U.S. Army 1st Infantry known as 'The Big Red One.' Except for seasoned officers, the soldiers consisted mainly of teenagers and young men barely in their twenties. The adults planned the mission and designed the training for the soldiers. The younger soldiers' responsibilities were to carry out the orders, execute the plan, and accomplish the mission.

The endless drills and rehearsals taught the soldiers to instinctively and unquestioningly obey orders – no matter how dangerous. Those with combat experience reinforced the lessons for the less experienced. Fortunately, the training included encouragement to think independently when confronted by unusual situations. They clearly understood the most important thing – to accomplish the mission regardless of the difficulties, discomforts, or obstacles. Known as 'Commander's Intent,' it describes the vision of how the battlefield looks at the conclusion of the mission. It empowers and guides the soldiers to initiate and improvise in chaotic, demanding, and dynamic environments.

When D-Day finally came on June 6, 1944, one historian noted afterwards, "None of these carefully planned and rehearsed activities even came close to working as planned and rehearsed. Not one."[20] As the infantry soldiers waded ashore the wind-swept beaches of Normandy, they encountered fierce resistance. Another historian noted, "The best planned, the best rehearsed, and the best supported invasion assault in history was falling on its face, mostly because of bad weather, partly because of the undetected placement by the Nazis of the 352nd Division. The generals were out of it now. If any of those GIs on the beach were to survive even the next hour, it was up to them alone. Every shield provided for their protection had been destroyed."[21]

They gallantly fought their way across open stretches of beaches, while many comrades lay killed or severely wounded. As the soldiers ascended narrow trails to the top of the bluffs above the beach, they braved land mines and barbed wire placed by the enemy to deter them. Then another obstacle loomed ahead.

One officer remembered how he was "surprised at the hedgerow and lane system that represented the bocage countryside of Normandy. We had not trained how to operate in this rather unusual terrain, nor were we even warned of its existence. It was strictly on-the-job training."[22] Another officer commented about the sturdiness of the hedgerows. He said, "They were of dirt and roots four to six feet high, with trees and shrubs growing out of them, tight enough to serve as fences that cattle and other farm animals could not get through." He also commented, "The farm roads were generally sunken between two of the hedgerows."[23] This terrain created conditions of fierce and tedious hand-to-hand combat with a well-entrenched enemy guarding these farm lane roads.

The soldiers instinctively knew that if they blindly stuck to the plan, they were doomed to fail. The cost would be their lives, the lives of those to follow, and perhaps the outcome of the war itself.

Because of the clarity of the mission, 2nd Division Sergeant Curtis G. Culin created an innovative solution. "By welding steel blades to a tank's hull, the tank would be able to crash through the hedgerow, taking dirt, trees, and roots with it – and creating a neat hole through which vehicles and troops could follow. The steel for hundreds of such 'hedge choppers' was readily available – on Omaha Beach. By working around the clock, welding crews jury-rigged the devices, which worked with remarkable efficiency – good old American know-how in action."[24]

25

The rest is history. The Allied invasion succeeded; Europe liberated; and the war's outcome determined. The younger soldiers' creative ingenuity achieved the mission, in spite of a plan that didn't go as planned.

This example illustrates an important lesson to consider. Flexible and creative thinking occurs more naturally when we're younger – think children or young soldiers. It's less natural when we're older – think adults or generals. We need to work harder as adults to master this building block.

Let's illustrate this concept in a different way. Dr. John Tickell is an Australian medical doctor and expert in stress management. He tells a story about an elementary school teacher on the first day of school. She works hard to learn all of her students' names. She asks Sally for her name and the profession of either working parent. Sally says her dad is a plumber. The teacher repeats her student's name, 'Sally,' and uses an association with a word related to plumbing and the same letter as the student's first name... in this case 'sink.' Then she asks Nancy, who says her mom is an accountant. The teacher repeats 'Nancy' and uses the association 'numbers.' Then the teacher asks Johnny, "What does your dad do?" Johnny replies, "My dad is dead." She replies, "Oh, I'm so sorry Johnny." And then she asks, "What did your dad do before he died?" Johnny holds his hand over his heart, tilts his head to the side, and replies, "He screamed, 'Aaarggghhh!'"

Did that answer catch you off guard? For most adults, it does. The answer doesn't fit into an adult's frame of reference. But kids typically say what they think, because they freely associate. Naturally playful and creative, they think with wide-open minds.

As adults, we often condition our thinking in linear ways. In today's world with so many competing demands, we search for logical and rational patterns to emerge. We develop prescribed thought patterns to cope with the multitude and complexity of situations and tasks we face every day. And sometimes those thought patterns are appropriate.

However, risks with that type of thinking also exist. It can limit our degree of openness and, therefore, our ability to see other possibilities. That limits our choices. As pressure increases, we typically think in narrower corridors. Too easily, we perceive things as 'black or white' and 'cut and dried.' When that happens, we eliminate possibilities.

Think of a blank white page without a mark on it. Without guidelines and under pressure, we often don't know where to start drawing. With kids' naturally open minds, they instinctively draw anywhere on the page rather than in prescribed patterns. A child looks at the same blank page and sees lots of creative 'white space' and immediately starts filling in a blank page of possibilities. That is... until they learn differently from adults.

So this strong conditioning causes us adults to need to work harder and stay open to new ideas and ways of thinking. Sometimes we need to avoid applying such a narrow focus in ways that prevent us from seeing beyond the end of our collective noses. Dr. Anonymous puts it this way, "If your nose is to the grindstone, the only thing you see is sparks."

When we ingrain too narrow thinking, we run an unfortunate risk. Potentially, we lose the joy of the playful and creative thinking patterns we experienced as children. That ties us to the status quo. An even worse consequence emerges when we then try to condition others to think as we do and in similar corridors. We need to guard against an over-dependence on logic. It potentially limits our possibilities and therefore our experiences and achievements.

Avoid any misinterpretations of my point here. I'm not against logic. I am against the use of logic *in the wrong times and places*. For example, when we try something new, explore possibilities, invent a new process or product, or need a creative spark when something isn't working out as planned, then rational and logical thinking may not lead us to the right path. In those types of situations, thinking too logically and rationally too early may prevent the exploration of options to find or create the right or best solution. That's why we must guard against prejudice, closed-mindedness, and blind protection of the status quo. We must remain open to new ways of thinking. As William James aptly put it, "Many people think they are thinking, when all they're doing is re-arranging their prejudices."[26]

I encourage you to stay open to other points of view. In no way should you abandon your beliefs. Simply stay open to discuss them. Strong beliefs survive scrutiny. They shape our self-concept.

With strong beliefs, your doubts have less power to override the actions you know you need to take. While we all have doubts that creep in from time to time, our beliefs enable us to overcome them, minimize fear, and maximize hope. Over time, your beliefs strengthen. When they no longer waver, they deepen into convictions. That's the C part of *The ABC Formula.*

Conviction

People are persuaded more by the depth of our own conviction than by the height of our knowledge.[27]
Cavett Robert, Professional Speaker

Conviction gives you courage to act decisively based on your attitudes and beliefs. Courage drives you to take action. It comes from your conviction's depth. *The ABC Formula's* framework is this: attitude is in your head; belief is in your heart; conviction is in your spirit. With it, your self-confidence increases. You act decisively, stand up to adversity, and follow through with resolve.

Let me give you an example. Ronald Reagan was the 40th U.S. President. In his biography, a fascinating story describes the air traffic controllers strike in 1981. In a cabinet meeting, Reagan's advisors hotly debated what to do about the strike. Both sides passionately advocated their positions. While the debate raged on, none noticed Reagan as he quietly wrote on a yellow pad.

Ronald Reagan held an unshakeable conviction: no civil servant had the right to walk out on the American people. In fact, the air traffic controllers swore an oath to never do this when hired. When Reagan finished his notes, he abruptly stopped the debate, ended the meeting, and walked into a White House press conference. Minutes later, he fired the striking air traffic controllers.

Ronald Reagan did not rely on research polls or town hall meetings to tell him what was right or wrong. He used his own moral compass to make decisions. Whether people agreed with his policies or not, they respected and admired his beliefs and convictions. Ronald Reagan clearly understood his definition of right and wrong. He acted with authenticity and congruence. After he fired the striking air traffic controllers, historians point to that event as the beginning of his real impact as president.

With Ronald Reagan, his actions followed his convictions. What you saw was what you got. My brother Norm was the same way. We counted on his counsel, wisdom, and actions. To paraphrase the television commercial from E.F. Hutton years ago, when he talked, everyone listened. He held deep convictions.

History provides us with many exemplary examples. Think of soldiers who die in defense of their nations' freedoms. Think of saints throughout the ages martyred for their faith. Dramatic acts such as these express deeply-held convictions.

But other less-dramatic expressions of conviction exist as well. Here's one. At a meeting, a person willingly voices an unpopular point-of-view against the majority opinion rather than remain silent. Is that an act of conviction? Of course!

Tragically, many people never act with conviction. Some say, "Do as I say, not as I do." That is *not* acting with conviction. As the Indian philosopher known for his stance of nonviolent protest, Mahatma Gandhi said, "A 'No' uttered from deepest conviction is better and greater than a 'Yes' merely uttered to please, or worse, to avoid trouble."[28]

When people act with conviction, their actions speak louder than words. *The ABC Formula* fuels their actions. Follow their lead.

Would others describe you as a person with deep convictions? Will you stand up or speak up for your convictions even if unpopular? Can others count on you? Do you always do what you say you're going to do? Those are hard questions to ask ourselves. They're also necessary for growth and development. It's clearly a choice to follow this path. Your convictions dictate your actions. They go a long way to make *The ABC Formula* a basis of your life. They define and develop who you are for all to see.

Start with changing your attitudes. That forms your beliefs. They deepen into convictions. *The ABC Formula* empowers and enables you to see possibilities. And possibilities need focus. That's why we all need a clearly defined purpose. It's your compass. It's the 'big picture' view of the *why* you do *what* you do. It's a shining beacon of light to point you in the right direction when darkness surrounds you. It helps you overcome short-term difficulties which appear to be overwhelming obstacles.

When Norm Cole founded Advanced Business Concepts, Inc., he defined our purpose with this mission statement: "To help business owners achieve the results they have always wanted from their businesses, and consequently from their lives." When I founded Advanced Business Solutions, Inc., my personal mission statement: "To positively impact people's lives," became our mission statement. It defines my passion and provides fuel to focus my actions and persevere through obstacles.

What drives you? What's your purpose? Do you have a personal mission statement? I challenge you to discover, define, or re-define your mission and purpose. Unleash a powerful force from deep within you to drive you forward. Without it, you risk acting inconsistently, like a ship without a rudder. With it, you gain many benefits including:

✓   Your attitude stays consistently positive.
✓   Your beliefs shine through.
✓   Your conviction drives consistent action in a specific direction.

✓ Specific activities define how to accomplish what is important to you.

✓ You measure your actions and their consistency with your purpose.

✓ Your energy increases.

✓ Others see a greater congruence in you.

Discover, define, or re-define your direction. Write an emotionally-charged statement for you to focus your thinking and therefore your journey. Avoid agonizing over the details. Eliminate any thought of procrastination. Simply write or refine a first draft of your Purpose or Personal Mission statement. Start with a few words. Begin now.

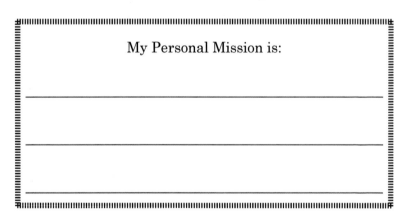

My Personal Mission is:

_____

_____

_____

As you translate your thoughts into a written draft, your journey starts anew. It takes emotional courage to accept this challenge. It's often a leap of faith! With it, you gain a significant purpose to drive your actions and pursue *The ABC Formula* in a meaningful way.

The journey will not always be smooth. You *will* face challenges. That's life. But now, you are better prepared to face those challenges... just as Captain Sully did on Flight 1549. You have a compass to guide you.

How to Fully Develop and Pursue
The ABC Formula

When you commit to develop, pursue, and apply *The ABC Formula* consistently in your life, you stretch, grow, and strengthen your attitudes, beliefs, and with time and experience, your convictions emerge. Your courage increases. Your resolve strengthens. Obstacles diminish, possibilities increase, and others view you as authentic and congruent.

In Part Two, I share more deeply my enduring Core Values and how they solidified for me when we lost Norm. Also, I share how they were forming even before that tragic event. But most importantly, I share what they mean to me now, and perhaps what they can mean for you.

As we travel this path together, we explore the *why* behind the personal importance of each of these enduring Core Values. Author and professional speaker, John G. Blumberg, articulated the importance of doing this. He said, "Asking 'why' of ourselves as we look into the mirror of our own core values can prove to be a powerful question that penetrates to our very core, thus revealing our truth!"[29]

Chapter Two Endnotes – The ABC Formula

1. Oliver Wendell Homes, Jr., *Collected Legal Papers*, (New York: Harcourt, Bruce, and Co., 1921), 292-3.
2. Rick Warren, *The Purpose-Driver Life: What on Earth am I Here For?* (Grand Rapids, MI: Zondervan, 2002), 265.
3. Lilless McPherson Shilling and Linda K. Fuller. *Dictionary of Quotations in Communications* (Westport, CN: Greenwood Press, 1997), 19.
4. Zig Ziglar. *The Ziglar Weekly Newsletter*, July 14, 2009 Edition 27 http://www.ziglar.com/newsletter/?tag=goal-setting.
5. Zig Ziglar, *See You at the Top* (Gretna, LA: Pelican Publishing Co., 1975), 209.
6. Harvey Mackay, United Features Syndicated Column, 3 Dec., 2009.
7. Barbara L. Fredrickson, interview by Frank Stazio, 23 Jun., 2009, *State of Things*, (North Carolina Public Radio WUNC-FM).
8. http://www.searchamelia.com/2009/08/31/smile-and-have-a-positive-attitude-on-the-job/.
9. Zig Ziglar, *See You at the Top* (Gretna, LA: Pelican Publishing Co., 1975), 202.
10. Towers Perrin Talent Report, *Working Today: Understanding What Drives Employee Engagement* (2003).
11. Towers Perrin Talent Report, *Working Today: Exploring Employees' Emotional Connections to their Jobs* (2003).
12. Wayne F. Cascio, *Economic Impact of Employee Behaviors on Organizational Performance* (California Management Review, summer 2006).
13. Recommend reading: Tom Bay and David Macpherson, *Change Your Attitude: Creating Success One Thought at a Time* (New Jersey: Career Press, 1998).
14. "Attitudes" is excerpted from the sermon, *Strengthening Your Grip on Attitudes*, (SYG7A) by Chuck Swindoll. Copyright ©1981 by Charles R. Swindoll, Inc. All rights reserved worldwide. Used by permission. The complete sermon can be heard on-line at www.insight.org.

15. Photo cropped from File: Plane crash into Hudson River. jpg (originally posted to Flickr as Plane crash into Hudson River (http://flickr.com/photos/22608787@N00/3200086900) on 15 January 2009 by Greg L. CC-BY Permission. http://commons.wikimedia.org/wiki/File:Plane_crash_into_Hudson_River_muchcropped.jpg, accessed July 23, 2011.
16. For this and other of Hubbard's witicisms, see www.brainyquote.com/quotes/authors/e/elbert_hubbard.html.
17. James Lane Allen. BrainyQuote.com, Xplore Inc, 2011. http://www.brainyquote.com/quotes/quotes/j/jameslanea194682.html, accessed September 11, 2011.
18. P. Kommers et al, *Cognitive Support for Learning* (The Netherlands: IOS Press, 2004), 171.
19. Henry Ford, *Dearborn Independent*, Vol 27 Issue 50, Dearborn Publishing Co., 1927.
20. Flint Whitlock, *The Fighting First: The Untold Story of the Big Red One on D-Day* (Cambridge MA: Westview Press, 2004), 139.
21. Edward Ellsberg, *The Far Shore* (New York: Dodd, Mead, 1960), 222-4.
22. Whitlock, 240.
23. Whitlock, 240-1.
24. Whitlock, 242.
25. Photo Courtesy of Colonel Robert R. McCormick Research Center of the 1st Infantry Division Museum at Cantigny in Brand – Whitlock, *The Fighting First*, 242.
26. William James. BrainyQuote.com, Xplore Inc, 2010. http://www.brainyquote.com/quotes/quotes/w/williamjam385574.html, accessed September 14, 2010.
27. Cavett Robert - http://www.cavettrobert.com/cavettism.html, accessed May 13, 2011.
28. Mahatma Gandhi, Thinkexist.com. http://thinkexist.com/quotation/a-no-uttered_from_the_deepest_conviction_is/216440.html accessed 1/30/11.
29. John G. Blumberg, *Good to the Core: Building Value with Values* (Naperville, IL: Simple Truths, 2009), 55.

PART TWO
CORE VALUES

Respect

Self-Control

Integrity

Service

Honesty

Work

Truth

Initiative

Accountability

Respect

*Probably no greater honor can come to another man
than the respect of his colleagues.*[1]
Cary Grant, Actor

Respect: it's something most of us want, need, or even crave. This common fundamental desire is a deep down, inside-your-soul yearning. That's why it's so natural for us to want to hold up others as role models. We so want to respect people in high profile and important roles. This includes parents, older siblings, teachers, coaches, business icons, religious leaders, politicians, sports heroes, and performers such as musicians, actors and media stars. So let me ask you this, are some roles more important than others?

Consider these: the person who picks up your garbage; the cook on a fast order grill; the landscape worker who cleans up the yards around the neighborhood; the teacher who works in a local school; the scientist who was just awarded a Nobel Prize; the lifeguard at the local pool on weekends; the stay-at-home parent responsible for a child's development; the worker who cleans public restrooms; the referee or umpire at a sporting event; the graduate assistant teaching at the university; the plant worker on a manufacturing line; the data clerk in the back office; the janitor at your fitness facility; the business owner who strives to remain competitive in a changing world; the telemarketer who calls you at work; the musician who plays at local dances; and the company's top salesperson.

Are all these roles equally important? Do you believe some are more important than others? Are there ones more or less important than yours? What's your honest opinion? Interesting questions, aren't they?

Early on, I learned a valuable lesson from my dad, Harold M. "Hal" Cole. Dad taught me never to underestimate the value of someone else's work. He said, "If you have difficulty respecting what someone does, try doing his work for a day." He believed when you take a turn in another person's shoes, you gain appreciation for the difficulties and challenges. You also gain insight into the important contributions made and gain a new found respect for the individual and the work being done.

Respect is an enduring Core Value. I believe *all* jobs and roles are important and deserve respect. Consider this. If a job exists and doesn't make an important contribution, then why is it there? In that scenario, there's no logic to its existence. Unless someone manufactures a job for some unique set of circumstances, then all jobs make important contributions and deserve respect. If you work in an organization and the president goes on vacation for two weeks, would you miss him or her very much if no one did the job? By comparison, if the person responsible for the cleanliness of your office and emptying the trash also went on vacation for two weeks and no one replaced him or her, who would you miss more? Sometimes, we underestimate the importance of what someone does for us until they're gone.

If a job or role makes a contribution, then the holder of each job or role is entitled to something else we all deserve: dignity. Grover Cleveland served two non-consecutive terms as the 22nd and 24th U.S. President. He's the only one to be counted twice. He said, "A truly American sentiment recognizes the dignity of labor and the fact that honor lies in honest toil."[2]

Jobs make contributions, deserve respect, and have dignity. That is so obvious, it's easy to overlook.

Here's a real-life illustration of how this building block works. Ken Wessner, a wise and successful businessman, based his career on the enduring Core Value of respect. He served as Chairman of ServiceMaster which, during his tenure and beyond, was often listed among the world's most admired corporations. Ken devoted an enormous amount of energy and commitment to the development of employees. He built ServiceMaster's business on niches in unglamorous markets. His employees mowed lawns and trimmed trees. They cleaned houses, mopped floors in hospitals, and served food in college cafeterias. He strongly believed in the dignity of every person. He also believed they deserved respect and learning opportunities.

Ken invested in his people with training and career development programs. This philosophy was not driven by tax breaks or government programs. He believed people are an organization's greatest asset, and he acted on that belief. In other words, it was his conviction. As a result, people who began in basic cleaning services grew to manage ServiceMaster business units. He's a great example of the application of the enduring Core Value of respect.

For me, and I hope for you, the lesson is simple. How can we not show respect for others when they contribute? How can we not show respect for others by giving them the dignity deserved for doing a job? To me, there is only one answer. All jobs earn and deserve our respect.

But there's another factor in play. To give respect, we must first have it for ourselves. This important aspect is a necessary ingredient in the equation.

Let's illustrate this with another story. One day, during his tenure as Governor of California and before he was the 40th U.S. President, Ronald Reagan strolled down a street in New York City with a newspaper reporter. Out of the blue, a man approached him eagerly with a pen and paper in hand. The man smiled broadly, looked Reagan in the eye, and said in a friendly pleading tone: "Please give me your autograph, Mr. Milland."

Mistaken for Ray Milland, another more famous American actor at the time, Ronald Reagan took the paper with a twinkle in his eye and cheerfully signed it, 'Ray Milland.' The man looked at his cherished autograph, thanked him for it, and walked away happy. The reporter asked Reagan why he didn't tell the man who he really was. Reagan said simply, "Why should I? I know who I am."

Ronald Reagan had a healthy level of self-respect. He knew who he was. So here's the point: self-respect leads you to respect others. In the Bible, Jesus gave us the Golden Rule: "Do unto others as you would have them do unto you."[3] It's about respect. And at the heart of respect is love. Frankie Byrne, a legendary Irish radio program hostess from 1963 to 1985, was known for her 'Dear Frankie' letters of advice. They were along the same vein as U.S. newspaper columnist Dear Abby. She once simply said, "Respect is love in plain clothes."[4] I agree.

Consider this. The next time someone asks for a moment of your time, regardless of that person's position in an organization or station in life, remember you've been sought out for a reason. Take a moment to find out what it is. We all want, need, crave, and deserve respect. Step into that person's shoes, even if it's just for a brief moment or two. You never know how important the moment is for the other person, or how important it will be for you. Even if you don't have much time, be considerate. It shows you care. As Zig

Ziglar said, "People don't care about what you know, until they know how much you care... about them."[5]

It's also important to understand how much impact can be made even in a brief encounter. I believe we can positively impact someone in a very brief time – particularly if the individual is viewed as a role model. This story illustrates the type of influence, and the impact we can have. In the 1920 Olympic Games, U.S. track and field sprinter Charlie Paddock won the gold medal in the 100-meter race. Called the 'fastest man in the world,' he returned home as a hero. In 1928, Paddock toured the country and spoke at a Cleveland high school. After his speech, a young student eagerly told Paddock that he too wanted to be an Olympic champion. Charlie Paddock encouraged the boy to give it his best and follow his dream. That boy remembered those kind words of encouragement. He became a very fast sprinter and eventually made the Olympic team. In 1936, he turned in one of the greatest performances in Olympic history. He captured four gold medals including the 100-meter dash and the long jump. His name was Jesse Owens.

When Jesse Owens returned to the U.S., he was also called the 'fastest man in the world' and hailed as a hero. In a motorcade honoring Owens, a young boy caught his eye, and Jesse acknowledged him. The boy excitedly ran home as fast as he could, burst through the door, and reported that he had just seen Jesse Owens. He proclaimed that he would be an Olympic champion just like him.

In 1941, Owens presented that same young man with a new pair of running spikes at an awards ceremony. That young man remembered the encouragement, used it as a source of inspiration, and later made the Olympic team. In 1948, he also won Olympic gold medals in the 100-meter dash and the sprint relay team. He added 2 more gold medals in the 1952 Olympics winning the 110-meter hurdles and was again a member of the sprint relay team. His name was Harrison Dillard. It's amazing how much impact we can have on others in a few brief moments.

Be encouraged to find opportunities to demonstrate how much you care. Jerome P. Fleischman, former editor of *The Rotarian*, said, "Most of us, swimming against the tides of trouble the world knows nothing about, need only a bit of praise or encouragement, and we'll make the goal. Say, 'Thank you!' whenever you think of it. Say, 'Nice job!' to that workman who put extra effort into his task. Say 'Atta boy!' to the fellow who is struggling through in the face of odds. You'll get a whale of a lot of joy out of life that way and people will love you."[6]

Notice Fleischman's use of the words *praise* and *encouragement*. To praise is to show appreciation, when it's sincere and true. If you're like most of us, it's unlikely you get shown too much appreciation. When someone does something nice for you, do you typically demonstrate too much appreciation? Or are you more likely to demonstrate not enough appreciation? How often do we let that good deed or special effort simply pass us by? Tragically, that happens much too often. What a shame!

By *not* showing appreciation, we ingrain the wrong habits of not praising and not encouraging others. That negative cycle of behavior by omission will not serve you or others well. When you omit or diminish these behaviors, you risk a diminished level of self-respect.

When you show appreciation, you demonstrate caring. When you demonstrate caring, you show respect for others. When you show respect, you build and reinforce an attitude of encouragement for others. When you encourage others, you impact people's lives in positive ways.

Seize your next opportunity to positively impact someone's life. If you need more rationale and justification, understand it's also in your self-interest. The Australian medical doctor mentioned before, Dr. John Tickell says when you say something nice or do something good for someone else, it pumps up his or her immune system. So actions that come from a sincere attitude of caring create a positive and physical response in our bodies. It might be just a small positive seed of a thought that counteracts a negative doubt – if even for just a moment. It might be something that turns a frown into a neutral facial position. Or it might just bring a small smile or even a huge belly laugh. But an improved physical response occurs.

Should we consider it a worthy calling to bring a moment of relief or joy to another person? Should we consider it a noble action to simply do something good for others, because it may lessen their burden for awhile? Of course we should! What's interesting is that your positive actions of encouragement often provoke reciprocal actions. It works something like this, "If you do something nice for me, I'll do something nice for you."

While that's not the reason *why* you should be nice to others, it's a good habit to develop. Did your parents tell you to be nice to others? Were you told to respect your elders? I know I was. How many of us allow those lessons to fade away or forget them entirely? You've heard those old sayings in countless variations many times before. But an old saying is often a good one. As Zig Ziglar said, "It's old because it's true. If it wasn't true, it'd be dead, because it would have outlived its usefulness."[7]

When we show appreciation, we encourage others. When we encourage others, we offer emotional support. When we give a timely and sincere "Thank you," it recognizes them for their efforts. That rewards them with a gain in self-respect. This feeling inspires them to persevere and try to do even better next time. Think of it this way. Life throws us all sufficient curves to challenge even the most self-respecting individuals. We all have moments of doubt. We all want, crave, deserve, and need respect, appreciation, and encouragement. We all need help to cope with the tough moments when they inevitably occur. Look for opportunities to encourage those around you. Make it a habit.

The enduring Core Value of respect underlies it all. When you give respect freely and in generous doses, you earn it back. Respect yourself and others. It demonstrates caring. Caring helps us reinforce and build up an attitude of appreciation. Show appreciation, acknowledge, respect, and encourage others. They reciprocate with kindness. These powerful acts encourage our mind, body, and spirit.

Respect: my dad, Hal, taught it to me and others. My brother, Norm, learned it and lived it. I aspire to this enduring Core Value daily. I implore you to as well.

Be Respectful of Everyone
You Come In Contact With.

Norman H. Cole

Chapter Three Endnotes – Respect

1. Cary Grant, Acceptance Speech Honorary Oscar, Academy Awards, 1970 http://www.youtube.com/watch?v=R0Zijgn-c9w, accessed September 14, 2010.
2. Grover Cleveland. BrainyQuote.com, Xplore Inc, 2010. http://www.brainyquote.com/quotes/quotes/g/groverclev118472.html, accessed September 14, 2010.
3. Lk 6:31 (NIV)
4. http://thinkexist.com/quotation/respect_is_love_in_plain_clothes/7397.html, accessed September 14, 2010.
5. Zig Ziglar, *How to Build Winning Relationships* (Krestcom Productions, Inc., 1994 video).
6. http://www.englishforums.com/English/JeromeFleishmanMostSwimmingAgainst/lnqxh/post.html, accessed September 14, 2010.
7. Zig Ziglar, *How to Become a Meaningful Specific* (Krestcom Productions, Inc., 1994 video).

Self-Control

*Like a city whose walls are broken down
is a man who lacks self-control.*[1]
Proverbs

What does self-control mean to you? It's a hard question, because for many of us, being out of control seems normal and being in control is the exception. Have you known people in a constant state of whiplash? People pulled in different directions wearing multiple hats? People struggling to cope with fast-paced lives filled with instant and constant communication? People stretched to the breaking point? People who have difficulty remembering when they were last in control? People who commonly complain about a lack of time? Sound familiar? The all-too-common complaint about a lack of time interests me. I love this saying from Dr. Anonymous: "The most successful person and the least successful person have one thing in common. They both have exactly the same amount of time."

If it's true we all have exactly the same amount of time, then time cannot possibly be the issue. While the popularity of the term *time management* exists, it mislabels the issue. How can we manage something that doesn't do anything differently under our direction or influence and is exactly the same for each one of us?

Time is simply... time. It's an asset to be used. And yet, we sometimes lose track of where the time goes and how we use it.

For example, in a typical life span of 80 years, we will spend 8 days telling dogs to lie down. We will be stuck in traffic 71 days. We will reprimand children 90 days – and that seems conservative to me! We will spend 621 days in the bathroom. We will spend another 1,825 days waiting for people. And finally, we will spend a grand total of 4,745 days watching TV!

In 80 years, we each have 4,160 weeks or 29,140 days including leap years. How many have you used? How many do you have left? There are 24 hours in each day. Those 80 years equal 699,360 hours. If we sleep approximately 8 hours each day, our usable asset of waking hours approximates 16 hours per day equaling 466,240 hours. How many have you used? How many do you have left? The 60 minutes in each hour equals 1,440 minutes per day with approximately 960 usable waking minutes. What's your plan for your waking minutes? The 57,600 available waking seconds today is an investment to use or possibly waste today. The clock is ticking! Time is our most elusive asset, and three fundamental truths define it. We cannot control time. We cannot save time. We cannot get time back once it's gone.

Time is an asset in which we invest... not manage. The real issue revolves around how you invest your time. What do you treasure? Does your time investment testify to what you *really* treasure? Time is a gift to be cherished. It should be invested wisely and appropriately.

The truth is, none of us know how much time we have left on this earth, as I painfully discovered with losing my brother Norm. So how will you use your time today? Imagine how you would approach today if it were your last day on earth. Would you do things differently?

After my mom, Beatrice "Kay" Cole passed away at the age of 88, my nephew Scott Semans gave her a great testimony that I used at her funeral. He said, "Grandma would make the same choice to do what she wanted to do tomorrow, whether she had a day, a week, or years to live. And that's what I love about her so much."

So how will this day unfold for you? Will it be in control or out of control? Do you have a strategy or a plan? Have you ever analyzed your approach to using this asset? Have you done it recently... in detail?

Let me challenge you to try this exercise. Track and describe the specific activities that occur throughout your day in specific chunks of time from when you get up in the morning until you go to bed at night. List the time you start on an activity and when you stop. Add up the minutes. Do this for each activity, and be diligent when you change to another activity. By charting the way you use your time during a day, you learn a tremendous amount about how you act in relation to what you treasure. That gives you data to create broad categories for your activities. To get the most out of this, repeat the analysis for several days or at least a day a week until you have an adequate sample of data. You'll be amazed at what you discover and learn.

As if it was yesterday, I distinctly remember my first coaching meeting with Gary many years ago. He owned a small business that consisted solely of five family members. I gave him this assignment and a form to use. In our follow up meeting, I asked him how it went. He told me he stopped after only two days. Before I said anything about him not meeting his commitment, I asked why. He said it was so obvious what was happening to him, that he immediately made significant changes. If you ask him today, he'll tell you it was at *that* precise moment he began to build a successful and profitable multi-location business. Gary took a leap of faith and gained the emotional courage to take on the challenge. He improved his self-control as he tracked and evaluated in detail how he treasured and invested his time. Most people discover between five and ten categories of activities. These tangibly illustrate how their time investment looks. Once completed, then it's easy to ask yourself if your time investment accurately relates to what's important in your life at the phase you're in. If you treasure and allocate your time and talent appropriately, congratulate yourself. If you don't, ask yourself why not? Through this understanding, we gain focus. We follow a more deliberate and specific direction. It allows us to move along a more specific path. My seven categories are Clients, Sales, Strategy, Commitments, Financial, Faith, and Personal. What are yours?

Those who complain about a lack of time do exactly the opposite. They spout off about some symptom as they release their inner tension. Unfortunately, they're not addressing the real issue, the *root cause* of what's going on. When we attempt to change a symptom rather than a root cause, no positive lasting effect occurs. The focus is wrong. That's why some people move in *reactive* directions while others move in *responsive* directions. What's the difference?

Here's an analogy. If your doctor gives you medication and your body *reacts* to it, it concerns the doctor. The prescription needs changing because of the negative reaction. On the other hand, if your body *responds* to the medication, it pleases the doctor because it's a positive sign. Our emotions work exactly the same way. They react or respond to a given situation. So how do we best keep our emotions in check and gain self-control? How do we harness our knowledge and apply our energy and focus properly? We must first address the real issue – not the symptom.

Now it's time for a disclaimer. I'm not a medical doctor, nor have I done any scientific research with hard data. But

I have worked with thousands of people in my career. As I observed people wrestling with these issues including myself over my career, I believe this chain of events creates this dilemma.

Here's what happens. When we feel out of control, it creates anxiety. When we feel anxiety, it creates tension. When we feel tense, it creates pressure which leads to a negative stress response. Unchecked negative stress responses lead to a feeling of depression. Unchecked feelings of depression lead to a state of mind I call *emotional bankruptcy*. Emotional bankruptcy often leads to types of negative addictive behavior.

On that downward spiral, folks share one thing in common: they blame external circumstances for their current, or even past, condition. I label it the *victim's belief syndrome*. This downward spiral leads to depression. It's all too predictable. Why? When people blame external sources, they create excuses. When they try to change something, or blame something over which they have no control, they lose the ability to initiate corrective action. We cannot change something *out there*.

To break through that downward spiral, we must first deal with *in here*, rather than with *out there*. Look internally first. It moves you along the path to gain self-control. Real answers exist inside, not outside. Understand this important building block and use it. It's a key life lesson.

When under pressure, I use a reinforcement tool to regain self-control. I clipped this short prayer from a Dear Abby newspaper column published years ago. Originally written by an American theologian, Reinhold Niebuhr, I later discovered the members of Alcoholics Anonymous commit this to memory in their recovery process. He wrote, "God, grant me the serenity to accept the things I cannot change, the courage to change the things I can, and the wisdom to know the difference."[2]

Notice how this adjusts and re-focuses our attention to examine the real issue. Rather than focus on what we can't control, we direct our emotional energy to what we can control. A Chinese philosopher, Lao-Tzu, echoes this same approach. He said, "He who gains victory over other men is strong; but he who gains victory over himself is all-powerful."[3]

Understand the real issue is not a lack of time or a victim of circumstance. Rather than focus on what we can't control, the real issues revolve around a lack of focus, direction, or priorities on what's important. To gain focus starts when we gain self-control. That leads to another important question: what creates self-control?

Let me share my perspective with some personal history. As a teenager, two outstanding high school teachers challenged me and expected my best effort. Both created environments that inspired me to excel.

Frank W. Poucher coached me in water polo and swimming. He built one of the top programs in Southern California at Whittier High School. In three decades of coaching, his teams won more than 80% of the time. Under his watchful eye, I set numerous swimming records. In my senior year, I gained recognition as team captain and won the most outstanding swimmer award.

Allan A. Trefry taught instrumental music. An exceptional musician and teacher, Allan built a top flight high school music program. As a quick side note, Allan also excelled as a collegiate diver. So we had the common bond of both music and sports. I played in band, orchestra, and jazz band. Under his guidance, I was student conductor of the orchestra, served as band president for two years, and won the most outstanding bandsman award.

I now appreciate how much music and sports share in

common. The requirements of self-discipline, practice, and performance all lead to self-control. My talents spilled over into other areas, and I was named to the honor society of Senators. By most definitions, I was a high achiever. Unfortunately, at the time I missed one key requirement. I lacked the same focus and discipline with my high school studies. While I excelled in music and sports and areas of service, I developed poor study habits. I simply did not apply myself diligently to my studies. At the time, I lacked self-control in that area.

I attained good to excellent grades by just being there and participating. By nature, I'm a quick conceptual learner. I got by on my smarts and my innate talents and ability. Deep inside, I knew I wasn't giving my studies my best. I can recall the argument inside my head. Busy with music and sports, I used the excuse that it was okay to procrastinate on homework assignments. Those poor study habits kept me from achieving my full academic potential in high school, even though I was always in the top classes. In spite of all that, I received the Cardinal Key – the highest award of recognition for a graduating senior. It was based on multiple categories of service, sports, leadership, community service, contributions to the school, and not just academics. I achieved a place of honor among the elite graduates.

My talents and achievements in music and sports opened doors to opportunities. Recruited by major colleges in both disciplines, my future looked bright. A leading collegiate swimming and water polo coach at UCLA, Bob Horn, also graduated from Whittier High and played as a teammate with my coach. The nationally-respected Director of Bands at UCLA, Dr. Clarence Sawhill, was my band director's collegiate teacher. Ultimately, I decided to follow the footsteps of my high school role models and enrolled at UCLA.

For three years, I juggled athletics, music, and academics. I did okay in music and sports, but academics created struggles. Those bad study habits finally caught up with me. To make matters worse, when a class or teacher didn't inspire me, I often stopped attending. Sometimes, I did not bother to drop the class. I missed one of the great lessons of all time, best articulated by movie actor, director, and producer Woody Allen. He said, "Eighty percent of success is showing up."[4]

My lack of personal discipline combined with bad study habits resulted in an ongoing academic struggle for three years. It also spilled over into other areas of my life. I did not perform anywhere near my potential in either music or sports. In year three, I fell on academic probation two quarters in a row. That caused me to be declared academically ineligible to continue at UCLA. I *flunked out* of college! For the first time, I failed at something. Ashamed and embarrassed, I kept it a secret from everyone – even my parents. This most significant crisis point burst into my young life.

In response, I joined the National Guard. After basic and advanced training, I arrived home without a clear focus and looked for ways to fill my time. I formed a rock band. I coached a local age group Amateur Athletic Union (AAU) swimming and water polo team. The following summer, I played in musicals for Allan Trefry at the local junior college and coached swimming and water polo for Frank Poucher. While successful at those endeavors, I felt unfulfilled and knew something was missing. In retrospect, I followed a behavioral pattern best characterized by Charles Schultz, the creator of the comic strip *Peanuts*. He voiced a philosophy through two of his characters. In one memorable strip, Linus advised Charlie Brown that he'd never known a problem so big that it couldn't be run away from.

After a year and a half of much soul-searching, I came to

the conclusion that I *really did* want to follow in the footsteps of my mentors and teach music and coach in high school. But I first needed a college degree and a teaching credential. That door was seemingly shut. So I made a choice and faced my personal crisis.

Did you know the words *crisis* and *decision* share the same Latin root? I find that interesting. *Crises* are specific, unexpected, and non-routine events that often create high levels of uncertainty. *Crises* test us in specific ways during emergencies or unexpected circumstances. That was certainly true for me. On the other hand, *decisions* are mental problem-solving processes that lead us to select choices from among alternatives. *Decisions* result in a course of action.

I now realize how often *crisis* and *decision* are linked together. My personal crisis led me to a critical decision. That decision led to actions which shaped my future. When approached correctly, a crisis can be a catalyst for a decision that leads to positive change. As professional speaker and university president Nido Qubein said, "Change brings opportunity."[5]

I decided to re-start my collegiate career. I enrolled as a freshman at Cal State Fullerton to focus on music. The reputation of the Director of Bands, Benton Minor, drew me there. A renowned and respected music teacher, I had met him years earlier, when I played Christmas carols at my high school band director's home. Although I didn't realize it at the time, Benton Minor and Allan Trefry were lifelong friends and classmates at UCLA. They both married in college. The two couples shared many dinners and evenings together.

Starting over for me wasn't easy. Old habits die hard. Even though energized by a new beginning in a new environment, I still slipped back into some bad habits. I did not practice my instrument enough. I did not perform up to my capabilities. In the first few weeks of my first semester, I occasionally missed classes. In spite of my new level of motivation, the pattern of behavior that hurt me academically at UCLA re-surfaced at Cal State Fullerton. Then a significant emotional event occurred. It's as vivid in my mind's eye, as if it were yesterday.

As I sat on the hallway floor outside of a music class that had not yet started, Benton Minor purposefully strode down the hallway. I swear he was looking for me. He stopped right in front of me and kicked my foot. He looked me square in the eye and said, "Bill, how come you've been missing your trumpet lessons?" Flabbergasted that Benton even knew my name or cared what I *wasn't* doing, I stammered some lame excuse. He didn't buy it for a minute. I don't recall exactly what he said to me, but I thought after he left, "Wow, I'd better watch out. This guy's paying attention. I guess I'd better start showing up."

For the first time in a long time, someone looked over my shoulder, or more precisely – directly into my eyes. I felt *seen* without a place to hide. Benton Minor took time to show me he cared. He confronted my behavior with the unusual act of kicking my foot. In fact, it was a wake-up call. It was also one of the defining moments in my life.

In his own way and in his own style, Benton taught me a powerful lesson that day. It is summed up well by Zig Ziglar who said, "Confronting a problem does not always bring a solution. But until you confront a problem, there can be no solution."[6]

When you confront a problem, a heavy weight lifts from your shoulders. Then you deal with the crisis. You make decisions rather than avoid them. Ultimately, a problem confronted leads to greater self-discipline. This building block puts you on the path to the enduring Core Value of self-control.

That memorable day, Benton helped me summon the

courage to confront poor choices and re-apply self-discipline in my life. To guard against slippage, I use a reinforcement quote daily from professional speaker, Jim Rohn, which I'll paraphrase. He said we all must endure one of two pains: the daily pain of discipline or the long-term pain of regret. The daily pain of discipline weighs ounces. The long-term pain of regret weighs tons.

This crucial choice of either the daily pain of self-discipline or the long-term pain of regret determines your path. The lack of self-discipline manifests itself in the lack of self-control. At the heart of the enduring Core Value of self-control is self-discipline. When you choose self-discipline, it moves you in a positive direction. It's a choice to make. Remember, our lives reflect the choices we make. Thousands of years ago, the Greek philosopher Aristotle said, "We are what we repeatedly do. Excellence, then, is not an act, but a habit."[7] In addition, the famous Green Bay Packers' football coach who won the first two Super Bowls, Vince Lombardi, said: "The quality of a person's life is in direct proportion to their commitment to excellence, regardless of their chosen field of endeavor."[8] A commitment to excellence requires self-discipline. The choice of self-discipline determines who we become. These building blocks are crucial.

Another favorite poem summarizes this philosophy. From an unknown author, it serves as a useful reminder. I share it with you as an important description of what we should all consider and reinforce.

> Be careful of your thoughts, for your thoughts become your words. Be careful of your words, for your words become your actions. Be careful of your actions, for your actions become your habits. Be careful of your habits, for your habits become your character. Be careful of your character, for your character becomes your destiny.

Let these words and phrases sink into your inner dialogue. Thoughts... words... actions... habits... character... destiny. These multiple self-disciplines intertwine with different elements of who we are and who we are to become. Our thoughts define our words which define our actions. Our actions become our habits. Our habits define our character. Our character determines our destiny. When you analyze this process of self-discipline and habit patterns, you look directly at what shapes you. As a best-selling author, Dr. Stephan R. Covey, said, "Our character is basically a composite of our habits. Because they are consistent, often unconscious patterns, they constantly, daily express our character."[9]

Our habits express our character. When we consistently exercise self-discipline and foster good habits, we gain control of our emotions. Self-discipline leads to the Core Value of self-control. Self-control helps us keep our emotions in check. Less successful people let their emotions control them. Successful people control their emotions.

Control your emotions, and it's easier to make the right choices whatever the circumstances. In control of your emotions, you maintain perspective. For many of us, it's so easy to get caught up in a 24/7 lifestyle and lose perspective. Sometimes we need to just slow down and take a deep breath. We need to develop more patience. Centuries ago, some simple and powerful words were written: "A man's wisdom gives him patience."[10]

Patience and perspective help us maintain balance and focus. Balance and focus help us gain wisdom. Instill self-control through self-discipline to develop good habits. Your thoughts, words, actions, habits, and character create your destiny. They all spring forth from the enduring Core Value of self-control.

Self-control requires work. And work, consistently applied with proper focus, produces results. That should be obvious, but we are often impatient people. Nothing good that lasts is accomplished without work. And consistent work over time produces endurance. Your habits do not happen by accident or chance. They do not happen when you try only once or twice. Built by work, patience, and endurance, your good habits condition you for excellence. Built on the enduring Core Value of self-control, good habits put you on the right path. The next step is to build the foundation for – and then maintain – the enduring Core Value of integrity which we'll explore next.

Be in Control of Yourself and
Maintain your Integrity.

Norman H. Cole

Chapter Four Endnotes – Self Control

1. Prv 25:28 (NIV)
2. Reinhold Niebuhr. BrainyQuote.com, Xplore Inc, 2010. http://www.brainyquote.com/quotes/quotes/r/ reinholdni100884.html, accessed December 4, 2010.
3. Lao-Tzu. QuoteCollection.com, 2010.
4. http://www.quotationcollection.com/tag/discipline/quotes
5. accessed December 4, 2010.
6. Woody Allen. BrainyQuote.com, Xplore Inc, 2010. http:// www.brainyquote.com/quotes/authors/w/woody_allen.html, accessed September 16, 2010.
7. Nido Qubein. BrainyQuote.com, Xplore Inc, 2011. http:// www.brainyquote.com/quotes/quotes/n/nidoqubein178330. html, accessed April 10, 2011.
8. Zig Ziglar, *How to Become a Meaningful Specific* (Krestcom Productions, Inc., 1994 video).
9. Aristotle. BrainyQuote.com, Xplore Inc, 2010. http:// www.brainyquote.com/quotes/authors/a/aristotle_7.html, accessed September 16, 2010.
10. Vince Lombardi. BrainyQuote.com, Xplore Inc, 2010. http:// www.brainyquote.com/quotes/authors/v/vince_lombardi_2. html, accessed September 16, 2010.
11. Stephen Covey. BrainyQuote.com, Xplore Inc, 2010. http:// www.brainyquote.com/quotes/quotes/s/stephencov132958. html, accessed September 16, 2010.
12. Prv 19:11 (NIV)

Integrity

*Integrity is the glue that holds
our way of life together.*[1]
Rev. Billy Graham, Pastor

The enduring Core Value of integrity closely connects to the enduring Core Value of self-control. With a greater breadth of perspective gained over the years, I now better understand why my brother Norm linked the two together. Let's start with a meaningful definition of integrity from Dr. Anonymous. He said, "Integrity is to know what you're going to do before you're confronted with the choice."

Our level of conviction defines our integrity. The C in *The ABC Formula* really counts here. Our convictions determine the consistency of our choices. They demonstrate our integrity with the choices we make. What you know deep inside defines your conviction. What others see reflects your integrity. Both must hold up equally well under pressure.

What happens when you confront a difficult choice? Would you champion a cause, even when it's unpopular? Would you fight for it regardless of the consequences? For just a moment, consider what is *really* important to you.

Under intense pressure, do you make good choices? A positive *yes* indicates you maintain integrity consistently. You consistently *walk your talk*. Your enduring Core Values guide your decisions. Unfortunately, many people realize an internal struggle occurs more often than they care to admit. When emotions take over under pressure caused by difficult situations and emotions dictate their actions, their actions contradict their stated Core Values. Those compromises expose an integrity *not* maintained. Unable or unwilling to *walk their talk*, the lack of integrity hurts their relationships.

This building block is both simple and profound. The presence or absence of enduring Core Values guides our actions. When we control our emotions, we maintain a better focus and make the right choices to take appropriate action. The Core Values of self-control and integrity are tied together.

When they are absent, people behave situationally on issues and *cater to the crowd*. Whatever course of action seems most popular for the moment determines their path. Sound familiar? Media reports consistently highlight this type of behavior in some public officials and career politicians.

People who are unable to maintain their integrity tell others whatever they believe their listeners want to hear. I believe it's a travesty when someone tries to make others feel good and satisfy their *felt needs* – when they do not fully believe in what they say. Avoid confusing style with principles. Over two hundred years ago, the 3rd U.S. President, Thomas Jefferson, advised, "In matters of style, swim with the current. In matters of principle, stand like a rock."[2]

Challenge yourself with this question: what principles do you hold so deeply help that you would never violate them? Your answer gives you insight into your enduring Core Values. These deeply-held convictions guide your actions like a compass. During stormy times in rough seas, we're challenged to stay the course. Times like these test our capabilities. They stretch our limits. When you navigate well through the tough times, you breeze through smooth waters. During an interview, the 39th U.S. President, Jimmy Carter also described this approach well. He quoted his high school teacher, "We must adjust to changing times and still hold to unchanging principles."[3]

In today's society, have we strayed far from this? Sadly, we easily see many examples of deviation from this standard. Think of business icons, political leaders, celebrities, and sports heroes who publicly embarrass us. Media reports bombard us with scandals involving sex, drugs, a lack of ethics, or the inappropriate use of power for self-gratification rather than for the benefit of others. In much of society, these behaviors underscore the rampant lack of two enduring Core Values: self-control and integrity.

A study of 1139 CEOs was published in the mid-1980s. Among the findings were that their number one priority was their families. They also said their number one asset was their integrity.[4] Would a similar study today yield the same results? It's unlikely.

A major U.S.-based CPA firm, KPMG LLP, conducted its 2008-2009 Integrity Survey. The results paralleled a prior study conducted in 2005. Employees surveyed in more than 1,500 firms were asked their perceptions of the CEO and other senior executives. The study asked employees to rate how well their leaders value ethics and integrity over short-term business goals. In 2005, 57% of the employees said their leaders valued them highly. In 2008, the number declined slightly to 56%. What these numbers mean to me is that *only* slightly over half of the leaders are perceived by their people as valuing ethics and integrity over short term goals. I believe this perception may be so prevalent because of a lack of humility. An attitude of humility grounds us in who we are, or at least who we should be. Other people see its presence or absence in their leaders.

Influential people who make lasting impacts are humble. They realize we all have weaknesses as well as strengths. One often counters the other. They realize their limitations. They view things in terms of the long-term good. Even though results matter, the *way* they compete is more important.

An exemplary example of this approach is John Wooden. The greatest coach in the history of college basketball in the United States, Wooden coached UCLA to ten NCAA championships in a twelve year period. He was the first person elected to the Basketball Hall of Fame as both a player and a coach. He once said, "It's what you learn after you know it all that counts."[5]

In spite of his many professional accomplishments, Wooden's attitude of humility characterized his life. All who knew him say that he was an even better person than he was a coach. He realized how much he still had to learn even after he reached the pinnacle of success in coaching. He humbled himself before others. He also said that values create an environment of integrity. So how do we develop our values? Look for positive role models to guide us.

As I grew up, my early role models were my parents and grandparents. They positively impacted my life. I was born on my grandfather Cole's seventy-eighth birthday, and a special bond between us was created. In fact, the nurses were confused when this older man showed up at the hospital shortly after my birth to check on the new baby. Mom fondly recalled the surprised look on the nurses' faces when they announced the visitor they assumed to be my father.

My grandfather, Perry O. Cole lived with our family for a few years after his wife passed away. He counterbalanced his strong love for family with high standards and principles. He strictly instilled discipline in his children and grandchildren. After graduation from Iowa Teacher's College, he pursued a teaching career primarily in public schools. He was as a teacher, school principal, and county superintendent of schools in Iowa before he moved his family to California. He ran for elected office in California for state superintendent of schools. He dedicated his life to teaching and serving others.

In my formative years, Grandpa steadily influenced me. He taught me about the importance of family. He once shared with me that his most difficult choice was between ministry and teaching. He felt called to teach. His passion for it was unquenchable because of its impact on people's lives. His teaching career spanned five decades. Countless students were impacted by him.

My grandfather's parents, John and Sarah Cole, were his role models. Although I never knew them personally, their strong values were evident in family history documents meticulously prepared by my grandfather. When my great-grandfather John E. Cole was thirty-three, he sought a better life for his family. He bundled up his wife, Sarah, and four children into a sleigh with all their earthly possessions. They crossed the frozen Mississippi River and staked a claim to homestead new farmland in Iowa.

They built a home and taught their children enduring Core Values. In my possession is a letter to my grandfather from his brother. He recalled the childhood story of being caught by his mother after eating strawberries from Mrs. Carmichael's garden on his way home from school. His mother promptly sent him to Mrs. Carmichael to ask forgiveness. He said that was his toughest assignment as a child. He closes his letter this way: "And a word for all the in-laws, grandchildren, etc., too numerous to mention individually. Share with me the genuine pride to have been one of a family whose integrity and fidelity to an exemplary life of influence from a lowly beginning in the soil of an Iowa farm. There is no better origin, and but few equal."[6]

My grandfather lived a positive and productive life. He raised a loving family of six children who carried on his enduring Core Values. In my early years, he influenced me significantly. At annual family picnics, we celebrated nineteen birthdays together. I cherish those memories. He passed away at the age of ninety-seven.

My parents, Harold and Kay Cole, were also wonderful role models. They raised three children including the last one (me) who was quite demanding and precocious. Early on, I developed the habit of rising early to eat with Mom and Dad. Every morning before Dad left for work, we ate breakfast together as a family. Dad also made a point to be home at the end of the day, so we ate dinner together as well in my pre-teen years.

One evening, a minister visited my family while Dad was absent. He commented to Mom about Dad's absence. She replied, "Do you spend *your* meals with *your* children?" He said no. She said Harold did, and left it at that.

Dad was great. He was always there for me. At the age of three, he taught me how to count by playing cribbage. That started my life-long love of games and contributed to my competitive streak.

One day, I learned the fascinating story about why he taught me to play cards and other games. As a teenager, Dad left high school before graduation to wildcat in the oil fields of Wyoming. Raised in a household where card playing was banned, the lure of card games beckoned. He learned a tough lesson as he lost some of his hard-earned wages due to inexperience. He vowed not to allow his kids to experience that same pain.

When he returned from his wildcatting experience, Dad worked for a major oil company. He toiled loyally for them for almost forty years. Although he was occasionally required to be holed-up in an office, he loved working outdoors in the oil fields. When he needed to work on a weekend, he took me along so we could be together. I learned the basics of driving in those oil fields. He used his time wisely. I always knew that he was there for me.

Mom had a full time stay-at-home job raising three children. My brother and sister actively participated in many activities during their school years, but their schedules were a breeze compared to mine. Mom was the key. Besides making an early morning breakfast for us every day at the crack of dawn, Mom chauffeured me to countless music lessons, swim practices, school events, and extracurricular activities. I never arrived late. Her remarkable organizational skills insured that. She also possessed incredible energy. I never lacked anything. My parents gave me every opportunity to pursue my interests. Thank you, Mom and Dad. What a blessing it was to be your child.

One attraction (among many!) of my wife-to-be Kristy was the enduring Core Values she learned from her parents, Bob and Doris Niemann. Among many attributes, Bob possesses self-discipline. As a civil engineer, he loyally worked with one organization for more than thirty years. He prioritized eating dinner with his family every night. He made himself available to help with homework, do projects, and teach his children well in their formative years.

Bob and Doris raised five wonderful children. In turn, they have been blessed with nineteen grandchildren and an ever-increasing number of great-grandchildren. It's impressive to hear the grandkids (even in jest) parrot back phrases they learned from Grandpa. This includes the famous buffet line comment necessary at family meals, "Take what you want, but eat what you take."

A few Christmases ago, the kids surprised the adults as they performed a play based on our family gatherings. Each kid took on a role as one of the adults. We roared with laughter. The kids nailed every nuance of our words and behaviors – including the flaws! Heed this advice: never underestimate kids. They absorb everything.

Those who know my mother-in-law, Doris, treasure her. Her deep love for her husband, children, grandchildren, great-grandchildren, friends, and God shines through her character. Her intelligence, quick-wit, and skill in languages provide great examples for others. Her caring attitude shines through all she does. She gives much of herself in service. Thank you, Bob and Doris, for your love and friendship for me and your daughter. You are truly great roles models.

Sometimes we underestimate the importance of our early role models. Their well-placed words and enduring Core Values shape who we become, particularly when we first become independent. When we're young, we don't give our parents enough credit. Have you noticed, like I have, how smart your parents became the older you get?

I was truly blessed with many positive role models throughout my life. And yet, not everyone is as fortunate as I was. Many grow up today without such positive role models. The good news is we're not stuck in a vacuum without good role models available. A respected educator, Dr. Tony Campola, spoke directly to this point. He said, "Your past is important but it is not nearly as important to your present as the way you see your future."[7]

There is much wisdom in what Dr. Campola said. Think of it this way. The way you see your future determines today's thinking. Today's thinking determines today's performance. Today's performance determines your future.

At critical turning points, we often don't know which path to follow. What is our normal choice in those situations? Do we try to figure it out on our own strength and with our own knowledge? Do we fear appearing inadequate, insecure, or foolish by asking for help or advice? Many people will hide inside themselves because of pride, ego, or some other factor.

Refuse to accept excuses that reinforce the *victim's belief syndrome* I mentioned earlier. Avoid the perception of being a *victim of circumstance*. Refuse to allow excuses to keep you from being all you're capable of becoming. If you need guidance, find positive role models. It's your responsibility to seek them out. They give us building blocks to guide our development. It may require some work to find other people and resources to guide you. But they exist in abundant supply. In addition to mentors, there are seminars, books, internet resources, and other technological resources to help you focus on who you want to become, not just on who you are. It's your responsibility to seek help and be ready to learn.

Learn this building block right now. Ask for help. It's not a sign of weakness. It's actually the opposite. When you ask for help, it strengthens your resolve, which strengthens your character. It builds more self-confidence, which enhances your self-respect. You gain a larger perspective as you gather input to make the most informed choice you can with the information you have. You also make better decisions and choices. Ken Blanchard co-authored the mega-successful business book, *The One-Minute Manager*. He stated this building block well when he said, "None of us is as smart as all of us."[8]

Get past any potential embarrassment of not knowing something or being 'thought-less-of' by not knowing an answer. Transition yourself from a pretend 'know-it-all' to a true seeker of knowledge with an eagerness to learn. How else will you find others willing and ready to help you? You may be surprised by how many people care about you and will take on that responsibility. Be encouraged by this axiom from Dr. Anonymous, "When the student is ready, the teacher will appear."

Take responsibility for your future. Be ready and receptive. That's your part of the deal. And so is asking questions. While many people will say there are *no* dumb questions, I disagree. My conclusion is, a dumb question is the one that's not asked.

I vividly remember a morning business networking meeting many years ago. Jerry sat across the table from me. We'd never met before. He recently purchased a travel agency. As he mentioned some challenges, I asked him a question. He thought for a moment, and then answered. I asked him another question. He hesitated, and then smiled. He said, "That's a really good question." He answered again. I followed up with still another question. He paused for several seconds of deep thought, and then grinned broadly. He said, "That's a great question. What do you do?" I said I worked with small business owners helping them build their businesses and have more fun doing it. Jerry responded in a matter-of-fact tone, "I need to become your Client." The student was ready.

At each critical moment in your journey, mentors will be there for you. It's your responsibility to reach out to them. Willing to invest time with you, they help you get the answers you need. You know them by the quality of their questions. Find these encouragers.

Throughout our lives, critical turning points shape our development and guide our journey in ways we can't possibly anticipate. Mentors and these building blocks guide the development of *The ABC Formula* based on your attitudes, beliefs, and convictions. They lead to your choices and guide your actions. You make better decisions for the right reasons. This process strengthens your enduring Core

Value of integrity. Its depth helps you maintain it.

When people express an interest to affiliate with me, I share my enduring Core Values. Before we decide to work together, I clearly communicate and they fully understand that a violation of any of these is non-negotiable and causes the termination of our relationship. They also know that these Core Values guide our decisions. If a decision based on a Core Value doesn't turn out well, they know I will support them one hundred percent. Good choices come from Core Values. Whether in business, school, church, relationships, or in life, enduring Core Values are the necessary building blocks to make good choices.

With them, people know they can count on you to act a certain way. They know you will not compromise or dismiss your enduring Core Values. They know you'll make a well-grounded decision before you're confronted with the choice.

Maintain your integrity and exercise self-control. When life confronts you with difficult daily choices, remember my brother's wise advice. Heed his counsel. It serves you well.

Be in Control of Yourself and
Maintain Your Integrity.

Norman H. Cole

Chapter Five Endnotes – Integrity

1. Rev. Billy Graham. http://www.lightfm.com.au/Financial-Advice/Integrity-The-Glue-That-Holds-Our-Life-Together. html, accessed January 3, 2011.
2. Thomas Jefferson. BrainyQuote.com, Xplore Inc, 2011. http://www.brainyquote.com/quotes/quotes/t/q121032.html, accessed January 3, 2011.
3. Jimmy Carter. BrainyQuote.com, Xplore Inc, 2011. http://www.brainyquote.com/quotes/quotes/j/jimmycarte110378. html, accessed January 3, 2011.
4. Zig Ziglar, *Building a Personal Success Foundation*, (Krestcom Productions, Inc., 2005 dvd).
5. John Wooden. BrainyQuote.com, Xplore Inc, 2011. http://www.brainyquote.com/quotes/quotes/j/johnwooden106379. html, accessed January 3, 2011.
6. Charles Grant Cole, letter to Perry Ogden Cole, July 1, 1951.
7. Tony Campolo. Great-Quotes.com, Gledhill Enterprises, 2011. http://www.great-quotes.com/quote/1201376, accessed May 20, 2011.
8. Ken Blanchard. http://sourcesofinsight.com/2008/12/31/lessons-learned-from-ken-blanchard/, accessed January 3, 2011.

Service

Business is a lot like tennis.
Those who don't serve well end up losing.
Dr. Anonymous

Remember the first *Back to the Future* movie starring Michael J. Fox and Christopher Lloyd? As a side-note, several scenes were shot at my alma mater, Whittier High School. If you missed it, I recommend it, if only for one brief and truly memorable scene.

When Michael J. Fox's character Marty McFly finds himself thrown back in time to the 1950's, he sees some amazing sights. When a car pulled into a service station, a team of uniformed attendants rushed out to the car. They surrounded it with a flurry of activity. They wiped windshields, cleaned tires, lifted the hood, and checked the fluids, while it filled with fuel. Along with the rest of the audience, I howled with laughter at that memorable movie moment. It reminded us what service used to be, and how unusual it is in today's world. When did we change terms from *service stations* to convenience marts? The importance of service seems diminished in today's world.

As a youngster, my brother offered me a job in his first business, a Texaco service station. The hourly wage was eighty-five cents. He said I'd stay in good shape, because no one walked on the job. He expected everyone to run and greet customers as cars pulled in. And Norm Cole led by example. He wanted customers to see the attitude of an eagerness to serve. And the key word is *see*.

One day, Norm realized that his customers could only see one part of the service provided. They saw the windows washed. A light bulb clicked in his mind's eye, as he saw an opportunity. He developed a checklist for each car. It guided the attendants to completely service each car. However, another even more important purpose guided its use. With the service completed, each attendant showed the checklist to each customer and reviewed it verbally.

The conversation sounded like this. "Here's what we did for you today. We filled your tank, washed your windows, checked the oil, the battery, and the air pressure on all your tires, plus the spare in the trunk. Everything's a-ok! Thanks for your business. We appreciate the opportunity to be of service to you today. Come again."

Did his customers feel well-served? Absolutely! What impact happened? Over the next few months, sales increased by 40%! The customer service checklist review process was the key. He proved that an eagerness to serve supported, by a good process, led to more business.

How many businesses today truly and eagerly serve their customers? Not enough! Many people talk about service. How often have you heard, "Good customer service is good for business?" It's a popular slogan, but it's rarely a consistent practice. Good service is too often the exception, and that's unfortunate. Good customer service done exceptionally well leads to an extraordinary environment.

Let me share one of my all-time favorite restaurant experiences. Kristy and I learned about a restaurant through good old-fashioned positive word-of-mouth advertising from another couple. They said it was a dining experience. It was expensive – but well worth it. Reservations were at a premium. The restaurant typically booked up six months in advance.

When we called for reservations, we politely received very specific instructions. Only one seating for dinner each night at 6:30 pm. Enter the restaurant from the back parking lot entrance.

When we arrived at 6:15 p.m., a small and nicely dressed crowd had assembled and an excited buzz of anticipation filled the air. Precisely on time as if on cue, the restaurant's back storm doors swung wide open. Two beautifully-dressed young ladies in long flowing gowns smiled broadly and greeted us warmly. As we entered through the storm doors and descended into the basement, they checked off our names on the reservation list. In our hands, they placed a pre-printed menu for the evening along with an elegant champagne flute. One young lady said, "Here's the menu for this evening. You're welcome to sip champagne and enjoy hors d'ouevres in the wine cellar. And be sure to ask our wine stewards for advice. They'll help you select any wines to enjoy with dinner."

As we glanced at the menu, we noticed nine courses listed with an *intermission!* A special evening beckoned. The other young lady poured champagne, which we eagerly accepted.

The basement was a converted wine cellar. Among the wine racks, beautiful trays of hors d'ouevres were set out for us and strategically scattered. The visual feast almost exceeded the culinary one. Hot puff pastries stuffed with soft cheese melted in our mouths. Fresh-shelled shrimp dipped in cocktail sauce burst with flavor. Fresh fruit, cheese slices, artichoke nibbler, and more rounded out the appetizers. I vividly recall the sights, smell, and tastes so many years later.

As we poked around the wine cellar, we noticed the retail wine prices. We quickly noted the stark contrast to typically marked-up restaurant prices. Unavoidably, we leapt to

mental calculations of how much money we'd save with each
wine. The more we bought, the more we'd save! How classic.
What great merchandising!

Two wine stewards answered questions and coached us
on what wines matched well with which courses. Orders
taken on small note pads insured the right wine would
show up precisely with the right course. We didn't need to
write a thing. We couldn't anyway because our hands were
full – one with a champagne glass and the other with our
delicious munchies!

After twenty-five minutes' exploration of every nook
and cranny in the wine cellar, the wine stewards invited
us upstairs to be seated at our tables. As our memorable
first course ended, we ascended the stairs into the main
parlor of an old Victorian-style house. As each party
checked in with one of the beautifully-dressed young ladies,
the other escorted us to our tables. As we settled into the
plush red leather-backed chairs, we noticed our names on
handwritten place cards which announced this as *our* table
for the evening.

Decorated with simple elegance, the physical layout of the
renovated house was unlike most restaurants. Several small
dining rooms dotted the first floor and enhanced our feeling
of coziness. As the fire burned warmly in the fireplace, we
felt like welcome guests in an English country home.

Just as we finished taking in our surroundings, the second
course arrived: a steaming-hot mushroom soup served
in large shallow bowls. The visual appeal was simple yet
elegant. As the pleasing aroma filled our nostrils, the first
sip surpassed all expectations. As soon as the 'licked clean'
bowls were cleared, the wine steward brought the first white
wine selected. With traditional ceremonial flair, he opened
it and poured a small sip for approval. With pleasure, he
proceeded to fill our glasses.

Then the third course arrived: a small elegant plate of

tender asparagus drizzled with lemon and extra virgin olive oil. Delicious! Course number four was a small piece of fresh fish poached delicately in a white wine sauce. A salad of mixed greens with a delicious vinaigrette dressing served as course number five. As we finished our last bite of salad, the ladies announced intermission and invited us to stretch our legs and view the upstairs art gallery.

After roaming through the upstairs gallery, we descended the back stairs into the kitchen. We observed the chefs as they happily prepared the final courses. We feasted our eyes on what was to come, asked a few questions, and eagerly returned to our table in anticipation of the next courses.

The sixth course, a grapefruit sorbet served in a champagne glass cleansed our palates. How refreshing! As we finished, the wine steward brought out the red wine selected for the main course. He opened it for proper breathing. The evening's centerpiece dish arrived: a perfectly-cooked medium rare Beef Wellington beautifully wrapped in puff pastry. Served with a flourish, it was absolutely superb.

After we devoured the main course, the dessert arrived: a lovely chocolate mousse. The final course (number nine!) consisted of a hot beverage with an offer of after-dinner drinks. Total elapsed dining time – three and one-half hours!

The leisurely evening passed by at a perfect pace. We never experienced any sense of being rushed or unnecessary waiting. It was our first memorable dining experience.

The restaurant owners built their business with a vision of great food combined with extraordinary service. We returned several times, and each time brought new friends with us. One evening, we reserved the wine cellar and celebrated a special occasion with a large group of special friends.

While the restaurant's business strategy centered on great food and service, it spun off another by-product. The special environment encouraged everyone who worked there to take 'ownership' of their customers. During the entire evening, management was invisible. The expectations created a special experience in such a way that everyone wanted to serve without the need for anyone to look over their shoulders.

After several visits, I calculated the restaurant's profitability. In 1980s-valued dollars, the owners' net profit exceeded $300,000 annually. They closed for two full months each year and vacationed in the south of France. What a business! It allowed them to not only fulfill their passion to serve great food in a memorable environment; it also fulfilled their passion for travel. Their business flourished.

When an attitude of service permeates an environment, it leads to unexpected opportunities. And it happens even when it appears that a customer doesn't want the service.

This story contains a great lesson. In the early 1900s, an elderly lady entered a department store in Ohio. The clerks immediately identified her as a "looker." Anyone with retail experience knows exactly what that means. After a couple of minutes, a young male clerk asked the lady, "May I help you?" She replied, "No thank you, young man. I just came in to look and get out of the rain."

How would you respond to that comment? Most of us would say, "Okay. If you need anything, I'll be over here. Just let me know if I can help." But this young clerk responded differently. He said, "May I get you a chair so you may rest a bit?" And she replied, "That would be very nice. Thank you."

After her brief respite from the rain, the lady got up to leave and the clerk noticed. He approached her and said, "Ma'am, may I help you across the street? Let me keep you out of the rain with this umbrella." She thanked him for his help. After he safely escorted her to the other side of the street, she asked his name.

A few weeks later, a letter arrived addressed to the store owner. A lady requested some furnishings for her home. She also requested that young man fill the order. The store owner wrote back to say he was sorry. The young man requested was not in that department. The store owner assigned his most experienced salesperson to serve her.

Another letter from the lady followed. Its firm tone was clear. There would be no order unless the requested young man personally filled the order. The store owner relented. Guess who wrote the letter: Andrew Carnegie's mother! At the time, he was the richest man in the world. The 'home' was Skiboo Castle in Scotland. The young clerk became a partner in the store.

What motivated that young man to act the way he did? Was he just lucky? Some might say so. Others would say he keenly identified a high potential buyer. I don't buy that. The young clerk simply cared for another human being and her comfort. Not for personal gain, not for a promotion opportunity, but because it felt right to serve and care for her.

The building block here goes beyond customer service. Develop an attitude to eagerly serve others in all walks of life. It builds excitement, teamwork, and community.

Compare this attitude to the stereotype of a salesperson who tries to sell you anything to make a buck. The real world works differently.

Let me share a personal experience. During a regional conference in Cancun, a business colleague invited me for lunch. He struggled for some time to be successful and asked me for advice. He told me about his reluctance to talk with a neighbor who owned a trucking company who could benefit from our service.

Upon hearing his story, I asked permission to tell him the truth as I saw it. He agreed. I said that if he was really convinced our product would help a friend, he should be eager to share it. I went on to say that since he experienced reluctance and discomfort, he was not sold himself. That was the real issue. I recommended that he stop selling until his belief increased. I told him to get more training, observe successful colleagues, or find more information.

He looked me in the eye and smiled. He said, "Bill, you're absolutely right. Thank you." The following quarter, his results turned around completely. He won the international top performer award.

I often say the most important sale is the one you make to yourself. If you are truly sold on what you do, you can't wait to offer it to your friends, your neighbors, your family, and anyone else you meet. What's inside you shines through to others. Sell yourself first.

This applies to more than work. Examine how you feel about your school, career, organization, product, hobby, or your church. How well does it compare to what someone can experience elsewhere? Will they find more happiness and fulfillment elsewhere?

When you're sold, enthusiasm follows. When you know they will experience something special, you pull for them to buy or switch. *The ABC Formula* shines through for others to see. Zig Ziglar says that from the moment you start to pull for someone to do something for *their* benefit rather than yours, you become *infinitely* more persuasive.

The building block is to do the right thing for the right reason. Whether there's an immediate benefit to you or not does not matter. Ask yourself, "What's truly best for the other person?" The answer is always the best choice to make. This lesson applies to sales or service. It also applies to life.

Norm often reminded me that in any interaction between

two human beings, one is buying and one is selling. And those roles may switch back and forth several times during the conversation. Now, I fully understand how true that is. If you lead a team of people, teach a child, negotiate with a teenager, participate in church or community activities, or participate in anything with a team of people – you already know a lot about sales. Life is about sales. Good selling starts with the development of the right attitude about serving.

In Grandpa Cole's autobiography written at the age of eighty, he said, "He seemed to picture life as a service to others rather than for selfish interests. This attitude no doubt led him to choose the vocation of teaching into which he felt God had led him." This influence – learned not only from my grandfather but also from my parents and brother – formed this attitude in me at an early age.

Develop an eagerness to serve others. Do it for the right reasons. With *The ABC Formula* at work, amazing things happen.

The enduring Core Value of service builds on and connects to the other Core Values of respect, self-control, and integrity. Strive for these fundamentals each and every day.

Be Willing to Serve Others and
Be There for the Right Reason.

Norman H. Cole

Honesty

*If you tell the truth,
you don't have to remember anything.*[1]
Mark Twain, Humorist

B eing honest isn't always easy. In fact, it's often difficult. Sometimes, we exaggerate or embellish the truth. Sometimes we put the most positive spin on things possible. Sometimes we try to impress someone. Sometimes we want to position ourselves ahead of the pack. Sometimes we try to avoid hurting someone's feelings. We fear the truth will not be well-received. So we back off and 'sugar-coat' what we say.

What causes us to do these things? For some, it might be motivated by a desire to please others. It might also be motivated by a desire to be perceived in the best possible light. But there's a deeper fundamental truth. We don't want to feel hurt. We fear the negative reaction to what we have to say. Remember what fear means? It's *false evidence appearing real.*

At the heart of this fear is a lack of self-respect. The famous author Virginia Woolf once said, "If you do not tell the truth about yourself, you cannot tell it about other people."[2] The truth starts with being honest with yourself. Only then is it possible to tell the truth to and about others. Until you develop the enduring Core Value of honesty, the

Core Values of respect and self-control are compromised. Without this one, we cannot fully embrace the other two.

Think of how many times – while you were waiting on the phone, or in a store, or in a restaurant – someone said, "It'll just be a minute," or "I'll be right with you." These common responses are rarely anything more than reflex statements. We hear them all the time and don't give them much thought. Yet they condition our patterns of behavior and reinforce that conditioning to others.

What if it *isn't* just a minute? This seems like such a minor thing. Yet your expectation was already framed by what you were told. Subconsciously, the longer wait causes you to glance at your watch. A small irritation forms. Over time, the effect compounds. It affects our own behavior. For example, some people think it's no big deal to ask an associate or a family member to cover for them when they don't want to do something at the time. Our inner voices justify this behavior with, "Little white lies can't hurt, can they?" Unfortunately, it *can* be a big deal.

What happens when a child answers the phone, and a parent decides that now is not the best time to talk. They say, "Tell them I'm not here." This can happen at work when you ask an assistant or co-worker to tell a customer or a vendor the same thing. Zig Ziglar says when you tell people to lie for you, you've taught them to lie to you.

Has something like this happened in your own experience? How many times? These actions contradict the enduring Core Value of honesty. Instead, develop the opposite habit and tell the truth. It's always the best thing to do.

Here's my personal testimony. As I described earlier, my collegiate career at UCLA is best described as a failure. I hid what happened from my parents, other family members, and friends. With my pride shattered, I was unable to share my shortcomings and too embarrassed to be honest.

After re-starting college at Cal State Fullerton, new opportunities beckoned. After the significant emotional event when Benton Minor confronted me for not going to my trumpet lessons, I worked harder on my craft. In a more focused way, I consistently practiced and applied myself. At the time, I participated in the second tier performing group which turned out to be a blessing in disguise. In the Concert Band, I met the love of my life and future wife, Kristy, who played bass clarinet.

When I wasn't dreaming of ways to spend more time with her during rehearsals, I paid close attention to Benton's conducting skills and rehearsal techniques. His musicality and depth of preparation impressed me. Not only was he an amazing conductor and teacher, his skills in organization and rehearsal management were awe-inspiring. My respect for him deepened significantly. As I practiced and applied myself more diligently, Benton encouraged me to audition for the top tier Wind Ensemble. He accepted me for the next semester.

At the Wind Ensemble's first rehearsal, my musical education took off. In that elite group, Benton demanded another level of excellence and commitment from each one of us. He stressed the importance of preparation to perform well by rehearsing well. Higher expectations formed new habits in me. I arrived early for rehearsals properly warmed up and ready to go. His expectations raised my level of performance. My personal expectations grew and reinforced new attitudes and habits. I observed the same with my peers. Friendly competition developed, camaraderie increased, and we drew closer through mutual respect.

As the hours of self-disciplined practice paid off with improved performance, I searched out additional performing opportunities. I played in the jazz ensemble. I performed in chamber groups. I won the first chair audition in the university orchestra. Benton hired me to play first chair trumpet with the Fullerton Civic Light Opera. I managed the semi-professional orchestra, and we performed many Broadway musicals independent from the university.

Benton also recruited a new faculty trumpet teacher, Jimmy Stamp. At the time, Jimmy was in his seventies and renowned as one of the finest trumpet teachers in the United States. The former trumpet soloist with the Minneapolis Symphony, he retired from recording studio work in Los Angeles to devote himself to his students. Benton presented me with the opportunity to study with Jimmy. What a fabulous experience it was to study with this incredible teacher and wonderful man. This became another life-defining moment for me. The pace of my improvement picked up dramatically. As the semester progressed, Benton assigned me the first trumpet chair in the Wind Ensemble for one piece, Malcolm Arnold's "Scottish Dances." At the time, the challenge intimidated me. In retrospect, I see how it was part of Benton's developmental plan for me. As we rehearsed, my confidence grew along with my performance capability. Things moved steadily in the right direction.

Then, at an afternoon rehearsal, Benton excitedly announced his invitation for Dr. Clarence Sawhill to guest conduct our spring concert in two weeks. A nationally-respected conductor, Dr. Sawhill was Benton's college band director. In his final year of teaching at UCLA before retirement, Benton wanted to honor him and pay tribute to this man who positively impacted his life.

That's precisely when the worst panic attack of my life occurred. For three years at UCLA, Dr. Sawhill was *my* band director. I studied conducting with him. Under his watchful eye, I conducted the UCLA Concert Band. He knew me well.

My closely-guarded secret was about to be found out. I had never mentioned my previous academic failure at UCLA to anyone except Kristy. But, if you can't be honest with the one you love, who can you be honest with?

Unless I walked away, there was no place to hide. When previously confronted with difficult situations not nearly this intense, that's exactly what I would have done. My habit was to withdraw and avoid. Would this personal crisis cause me to run away and hide again?

I mentioned before that the words *crisis* and *decision* come from the same Latin root. It's interesting how often one leads to the other. My personal crisis confronted me with a serious choice. A decision loomed and needed to be made quickly.

If I repeated my normal pattern of withdrawal and avoidance, I would lose any progress made and slide backwards. What would happen to all the hours of hard work I put in the practice room and rehearsals? Instinctively, I knew that the consequences of this decision were huge.

This realization hit me like a ton of bricks. Rarely do avoidance behaviors work out for the best. They never solve a problem. They only make things worse. As this concept locked in, a new understanding formed in me. I realized that change was necessary. I became open to search for ways to follow some advice from author and civil rights activist, James Baldwin. He said, "Not everything that is faced can be changed. But nothing can be changed until it is faced."[3]

I readied myself to face this crisis. Deep inside, I knew I needed help. This was bigger than what I could take care of on my own. Who should I reach out to and trust with my closely-guarded secret? There really was only one choice: Benton Minor. I asked myself, "Could Benton Minor help me?" The answer was, "Of course he *could* help me. The real question was *would* he help me?"

I considered how he might react to my disclosure. I respected this man. He demonstrated his care for me, when he confronted my behavior of missed trumpet lessons. He challenged me. He encouraged me. He presented me with opportunities.

In my mind, only two questions remained. Could I overcome my fears and ask for help? Could this difficult situation be resolved? What would you do? Would you avoid it or resolutely meet it head on?

My personal crisis presented an opportunity to learn another building block. It's embedded in a phrase once stated by Albert Einstein. He said, "In the middle of difficulty lies opportunity."[4] I realized there was no way to avoid the situation or take it on alone. Those options didn't make any sense to me. Not this time! I decided to take a chance on my future. I decided to put my trust in full disclosure and confide in Benton Minor.

I summoned up courage late the next afternoon and found Benton in his office. As I stood in the doorway, he laid down his pen and gave me his full attention. He instinctively knew that I needed to discuss something important. He invited me into his office to sit down. As I nervously told him about my past academic troubles at UCLA, Benton listened intently and carefully to my story. He didn't interrupt me with lots of questions.

It was the most difficult conversation of my life. It was also a cleansing experience. As I finished, I felt a tremendous load lifted off my shoulders. I understood, with great clarity, a principle well-stated in this old Swedish proverb: "Shared joy is double joy; shared sorrow is half a sorrow."[5]

When I finished, Benton said, "Bill, don't worry. We'd hate to lose you now. I'll make some confidential inquiries on your behalf and let you know what we should do." Did you notice he used *we* twice? *We* is incredibly more powerful than *I*. This moment shaped and re-defined me. I no longer felt alone. Support was there with someone right alongside me.

Benton followed through exactly as he said he would do. He inquired confidentially on my behalf. He reported back to me. Surprisingly, what I did was not unprecedented. The fact that I'd come to him with my burden was in my favor. Benton advocated on my behalf with the administration. He evaluated my UCLA academic transcripts. Due to his efforts, my academic status upgraded from a second semester freshman to a second semester junior. In essence, Benton salvaged two years of my past efforts at UCLA and significantly shortened my graduation requirements. His precious gift positively impacted my life in a major way. What a boost!

My choice to confide in Benton Minor was a critical turning point for me. I learned a powerful lesson that locked in this fundamental building block. It's well-stated by Nido Qubein: "You and I today are the sum total of the choices that you and I have made in our life up to this point."[6]

Within a year and a half, I graduated with a Bachelor of Music Degree. In the Music Department, I won the Outstanding Senior award. Two years later, I received a double Master of Arts degree in Trumpet Performance and Instrumental Conducting. I was the first Masters Degree graduate in both fields at California State University, Fullerton. Benton Minor initiated both degree programs specifically for me. I graduated with honors.

What Benton did for me was above and beyond a normal bond created between student and teacher. He supported an insecure young adult in need. At a critical turning point in my life, his care and compassion boosted my self-confidence, self-respect, and self-esteem. I daily celebrate the impact he made not only on me, but on the lives of so many others.

Thank you, Benton Minor, for your dedication to your students. Thank you for challenging us with opportunities to pursue our dreams. Thank you for your pursuit of excellence. Thank you for how deeply you impacted my life. I deeply respect and admire you. You enriched my life in so many ways. I consider you one of my most significant mentors.

Fortunately, I gave Benton this message before he passed away a few years ago. Today, his legacy *lives on* in his students who have their own stories and memories. He touched many lives deeply.

So let's review what happened. Tested in new ways, I confronted my personal crisis. I dealt with this situation in a way that enhanced my self-perception. As a result, my self-concept strengthened. Ultimately, it led me to a deeper level of self-respect. Of the many lessons learned through this experience, the one that tops the list is perhaps the simplest building block. As Dr. Anonymous says, "Honesty is always the best policy."

While simple to understand, it's often difficult to implement. Why is that? A major reason that telling the truth is difficult is because it may be painful in the moment. The old saying, "The truth hurts," may be true. But when you consider whether or not you should be truthful, ask these other questions. Who *really* gets hurt by the truth? Is it the other person or *me*? What's the *consequence* of telling the truth? What's the consequence of *avoiding* the truth?

To determine the appropriate course of action, examine your intent. Are you trying to resolve something, get it behind you, and build someone up in the process? If so, then move forward and work on the most effective way to deliver the message.

If, on the other hand, there is a risk of tearing someone down, then re-examine your motives. What is the issue? Do you really understand it? How can it best be addressed? What happens if it's not addressed? Are you the best person to address it? These questions will help you understand your intent and examine your motives. That's a key step, because we may damage or enhance someone's self concept by telling the truth with the right or wrong intent or approach.

As your self-concept strengthens, you accept weaknesses as something to work on. In that frame of mind, we build up others... and ourselves. We are, after all, only human. We all possess egos. While there's nothing wrong with a strong ego, it needs to be channeled properly. Sometimes, we need to get our egos out of our way. I once heard that a person spends the first half of his life building an ego, and the second half shedding it. Wouldn't it be better to shed the negative aspects of our ego sooner than later? *That* signals a person's maturity.

As you prepare to be honest with someone, it requires this new level of maturity. When you do, you reach a deeper level of maturity and honesty best characterized by the word *transparent*.

When Norm first used this word in this context with me, I did not fully understand it. What does transparent mean? When you look at transparent plastic or a glass cover, you see right through it. Nothing is hidden. You see the blemishes and imperfections. Transparent people are the same way. They're totally open. No hidden agendas exist.

Let me share another example from my good friend, Diamond Dave Curry. In his seminars, one organization's management team gave him high ratings and positive feedback with the exception of one person. Dave needed to confront the problem with the one negative participant. He scheduled a meeting with the president to address the issue.

When they met, Dave was transparent. He felt the one exception negatively impacted the others. He said that he believed it was in their best interests to replace that person.

The president agreed with Dave, since *he* was the negative participant. For whatever reason, he didn't relate well to the training. He also knew that his people benefitted. He knew he needed to get out of the way. Did it take guts to deliver the bad news? Of course it did. That's one reason why I deeply admire and respect Diamond Dave Curry. I value him as a colleague.

Dave provided a great example of the old saying: "Be brutally honest." But be brutally honest with the intent of building someone up rather than tearing someone down. Your intent plays the paramount role. Be brutally honest *only* when your intent is to build up. That's transparency at its best. It's always the best policy.

Unfortunately, one occupation earns the reputation just the opposite of this enduring Core Value. In politics, particularly in the United States, the perception is that the best way to win an election or get things done is to tear down the opposition, and therefore look better by comparison. Ignore those high profile politicians. Behavior like that is better left undone. It's the opposite of being a positive role model. Avoid criticism with the intent to tear down. It can become a habit. We need to first look hard at ourselves and then act accordingly. Follow this teaching by Jesus: "If any one of you is without sin, let him be the first to throw a stone."[7]

With transparency, you recognize your weaknesses. With transparency, others see how to best help you. This degree of truthfulness requires you to humble yourself. With this enduring Core Value to guide you, a willingness to work on those weaknesses develops. With that spirit, then – and only then – do you earn the right to help others.

My great uncle, Franklin J. Cole, was a California Superior Court Judge. I inherited his daily devotional. It contains a wonderful poem written by Dr. Anonymous. It says, "There is so much bad in the best of us, and so much good in the worst of us, that it behooves each one of us to be charitable to the rest of us."[8]

Take this spirit of humbleness to heart. Develop humility. Open your life to others and be transparent. This locks in the enduring Core Value of honesty. Apply this building block in your life from this moment forward.

Be Totally Honest and Transparent.

Norman H. Cole

Chapter Seven Endnotes – Honesty

1. Mark Twain. BrainyQuote.com, Xplore Inc, 2011. http://www.brainyquote.com/quotes/quotes/m/marktwain133066.html, accessed January 3, 2011.
2. Virginia Woolf. BrainyQuote.com, Xplore Inc, 2011. http://www.brainyquote.com/quotes/quotes/v/virginiawo131850.html, accessed January 3, 2011.
3. http://www.great-quotes.com/quote/818927, accessed January 3, 2011.
4. Albert Einstein. Thinkexist.com, 2011. http://thinkexist.com/quotation/in_the_middle_of_difficulty_lies_opportunity/10122.html, accessed January 3, 2011.
5. http://thinkexist.com/quotation/shared_joy_is_a_double_joy-shared_sorrow_is_half/176839.html, accessed January 3, 2011.
6. Nido Qubein, How to Educate... not just Train... Employees (Krestcom Productions, Inc. 1994 video)
7. Jn 8:7 (NIV)
8. Franklin J. Cole, personal papers in possession of the author.

Work

*Sometimes you need to do what you have to do
in order to do what you want to do.*
Dr. Anonymous

An unfair label exists for the younger generations of workers. Some classify the younger generation as *slackers*. A perception persists they lack a good work ethic. That's unfair and biased. Many young folks possess great work ethics. While there certainly are those who slack off, both types of work ethics operate in today's society. The younger generation simply differs from the previous generation. And the previous generation differed from its previous generation. And so goes the world.

For generations, parents, grandparents, and great-grandparents endured and embraced hard work. In the Great Depression of the 1930s, there was no choice but to work hard. The ongoing struggle challenged the twenty-five percent of the U.S. population out of work. To keep food on the table and provide stability in difficult times, hard work was paramount.

Many grew up on a farm, or were only a generation removed from it. On a farm, work defined the day. It started early. Remember the phrase, "early to bed, early to rise?" That lifestyle defined and conditioned earlier societies. As we moved from a farm-based society to a manufacturing society, those early risers transitioned to the early shift in the factories. They clocked in on time, put their backs into repetitive work, took breaks only when told to do so, and clocked out at the end of the shift. Another old saying was "All I ask is an honest day's work for an honest day's pay." That defined work.

As farming receded during the progression of the industrial age, more people moved to the cities for opportunities created by manufacturers. Multiple shifts added more jobs as the economy grew. Some worked the night shift. As work patterns changed, the services sector of the economy developed to meet the rising demand.

In today's information-based society, the norms again have shifted dramatically. We see a movement away from standard work schedules and strict environments to more flexible ones. Many access and accomplish work in places other than a central office and at different times. On one hand, technology sets us free. On the other hand, it ties us to work 24/7 with demands for connections and accessibility.

For those raised in more structured traditional environments, their perspective differs dramatically from those exposed to non-traditional environments. No wonder friction exists between the generations of workers with such different frames of reference. We should avoid judgments of the younger generation based on patterns imposed by other generations.

As an example, my parents helped form my work ethic. Their early-rising habit conditioned my behavior. In fact, Mom and Dad met through 5:30 a.m. phone calls between the office and the oilfields. As she answered those early morning phone calls, she'd hear, "Good Morning Sunshine!" She claimed his sunny disposition at such an early hour irritated her. I don't believe that for a moment. More likely, she cherished those early morning calls.

Mom and Dad were athletes in their youths. Both played

baseball, Dad ran track, and Mom played basketball. We belonged to the YMCA as a family. I fondly remember Friday Y Family Nights filled with badminton and swimming. I learned to swim, before I learned to walk.

When I started on the Y swim team at the age of nine, I was not competitive. The first four years, I showed up and participated. When my adolescent growth spurt occurred at the age of thirteen (I grew seven and a half inches in less than three summer months), the workouts paid off. I improved rapidly. That motivated me to practice with greater intensity. The increased intensity resulted in greater speed.

In eighth grade, I won a few events on the Y team and won the most improved swimmer award and was named honorary team captain. I felt proud of my improvement, even with the modest level of competition.

That summer, I joined the Whittier Swim Association, a successful Amateur Athletic Union (AAU) age group team. I vividly remember my first workout. I dove into the pool in the outside lane and started swimming at what I considered to be a fast pace. A girl half my size with a buzz saw stroke ripped past me in the next lane. I increased my stroke intensity and strained to catch her. Instead, the splash of her flutter kick disappeared as she moved faster and farther away from me. What a rude awakening! That tough lesson set back my cocky thirteen year old ego a bit! Welcome to the world of competitive swimming. I just got introduced to a new teammate, nine-year-old Gretchen Lenzen. In her age group, she held the national record for the 100-yard freestyle.

Immediately, I realized the new level of effort required. I applied myself diligently. I swam additional workouts in the early mornings and longer practices in the afternoon. The hard work paid off, and I consistently won races. I loved the competition. And yes, I even beat Gretchen later that summer. My days were filled with long practices requiring dedication, intense effort, and hard work.

When I started high school, swimming was a passion. I set school records as a freshman. Dad built me a customized medal and trophy case to hold my cache of medals and trophies and installed it in my bedroom. My swimming success paid off with more opportunities.

The city of Whittier hired me as a Junior Lifeguard for the summer after my freshman year at the age of fourteen. My princely pay was $1.15 per hour. For two summers, I washed decks, taught swimming lessons, and saved a few kids from drowning. In the mornings, I taught swimming and worked extra shifts as a lifeguard – sometimes until nine o'clock in the evening. After my second summer, the city recognized me with the Tom Harlan award as the Outstanding Junior Lifeguard based on my service and willingness to work.

My swimming steadily improved. I won a California Interscholastic Federation (CIF) high school championship and also a Southern California AAU Junior Olympic Championship. I played on championship water polo teams. My work ethic formed and laid the foundation for future successes.

Let's look at the building blocks from these events and how to apply them. To develop your work ethic, start with a willingness to try something new. That's phase one. When I started on the Y swim team, I was not particularly good. But I stuck with it. It takes time for the consistency of practice to take effect. That's phase two. Then comes the point where you decide to move to a new level, as I did with the AAU swim team. That first workout served as a big wake-up call. I realized the new level of effort required. That's phase three.

Coaches, teachers, mentors, or other supporters guide your development in phase four. Your willingness to be coached and accept or ask for help means a lot here. Also required is patience. It takes time before something becomes comfortable and routine. With talent, progress occurs.

Phase five begins when external factors motivate you. In swimming, the reward initially was to improve your best time. So was an encouraging word from the coach. Then winning a race became the reward. Ribbons, medals, and trophies added another level of recognition. These external rewards and forms of recognition reinforced my willingness to work hard.

These principles certainly apply in environments other than sports. For example, in music, learning a new piece of music is a reward. Positive feedback received from your teacher recognizes your progress. At the end of a well-performed piece, applause both rewards and recognizes your efforts. Over time, the need diminishes for external rewards or recognitions – although they're always nice to receive!

This sets the stage for phase six. When your internal drive surfaces, you find joy in what you do. The motivational drive pendulum swings from primarily external to primarily internal factors. When that happens, your motivational drive kicks in and you do things for your reasons and not for others.

When well-managed, phase seven builds the habit of self-discipline. Your level of focus, determination, dedication, and preparation increases. Your skill level advances. Hard work pays off with opportunities.

My swimming success led me to also be a fairly good water polo player. If you don't know much about water polo, think in terms of a fast-paced combination of soccer, ice hockey, and a seal-juggling act. The rules prohibit you from touching the pool bottom or side walls. To rest in water polo means to tread water. It's a strenuous sport. I played on excellent high school championship teams.

As a sophomore, I played in the Junior Nationals Water

Polo tournament and met UCLA coach, Bob Horn. He started a recruitment campaign then for me to play for him when I graduated from high school. Sports and music led me to many opportunities. But the most long-lasting effect on my career was learning the importance of preparation. Here's what I mean. The all-time leader in men's NCAA collegiate basketball coaching wins was interviewed early in his career during a segment on the long-running TV program *60 Minutes*. As coach of the national champion Indiana University men's basketball team, Bobby Knight shared this insight. He said, "The will to succeed is important. But I'll tell you what's even more important. It's the will to prepare."[1]

As a sophomore at UCLA, I earned a spot on the varsity water polo team. I'll be the first to admit that my UCLA athletic career was not anything to brag about. I never achieved my full potential. However, one brief shining moment taught me a valuable lesson about the willingness to work and prepare. I hope it provides the same meaning for you.

In the showdown game for the Pac 8 championship (it's now the Pac 12 – that shows you how old I am), we played Cal at Berkeley. The game was a nail-biter – tied eight-to-eight in the final minute of play. By the way, that game was the only one my parents were able to attend all season.

As I cheered from the bench and with only twenty-four seconds to play, my teammate – the collegiate player of the year, Torrey Webb – scored a goal to put us ahead nine to eight! Our excitement spilled over.

But Cal wasn't through yet. The unthinkable happened. With only seven seconds to play, Torrey Webb fouled out. The referee gave Cal the ball right in front of our goal. Coach Horn looked down the bench and said, "Bill, get in there. Just play defense out on the perimeter. Don't worry about anything else." I admit that I was *worried* and more than a little *nervous.*

I dove into the pool with just seven seconds left, swimming to guard my man on the perimeter. Play started. Five seconds later, Cal scored. The Cal fans erupted in pandemonium. The Cal players on the bench were on their feet cheering wildly. With the score tied nine-to-nine, with only two seconds to play, and without our star player, overtime loomed.

Our well-coached team had a deep tradition of success. To give you perspective, you've most likely heard of Kareem Abdul Jabbar. When he retired from professional basketball, he headed the list of all-time scoring leaders in the history of the NBA. Formerly known as Lew Alcindor, he played at UCLA for the John Wooden-coached basketball team in the same era I played water polo. One of the most dominant collegiate teams of all time, Lew Alcindor's basketball team won three consecutive national championships. At one point, that team won forty-seven consecutive games. Our UCLA water polo team won fifty-four consecutive games over four seasons – a longer winning streak than Alcindor's basketball team.

With only two seconds left in our game, my conditioning for success took over at this crucial point – gained from hundreds of hours of practice. I swam to my normal position at half court at the left side of the pool. We set up our Double X play. Then an unexpected opportunity occurred. My guard temporarily lost focus on the game situation. He continued to celebrate the last goal scored. With two seconds left to play, I was at half court near the left side of the pool with no one closely guarding me. The referee threw the ball to our goalie to re-start play. He saw me open and threw me the ball. I caught it, whirled around, and looked at the Cal goalie. He moved towards me to protect the closest side of the goal. I took a deep breath, scissor-kicked my legs with a strong egg-beater that lifted my shoulders up out of the water, and just let it fly with all my strength.

Vividly, I still see in my mind's eye the goalie diving to my right (his left) from the side of the goal. The ball went *just past* his outstretched fingertips. It hit the back of the net just inside the upper right corner of the goal just as the gun went off. My shot was good, and we won the championship game ten-to-nine! That's the last thing I saw, because the entire UCLA bench jumped directly onto me in the pool.

After the game, one teammate commented I made a lucky shot. The truth is… it was *not* a lucky shot. Because of my strong arm, my high school coach designed a half court play for me. I spent hours in practice shooting and making half court shots. I made dozens of shots in games before that specific opportunity occurred. No luck was involved in making that shot.

Here's the point. That two-second opportunity came after thousands of hours of practice. Years of hard work paid off. When you condition yourself for success, you create chances to be in the right place at the right time with the opportunity to succeed. You just never know when it might occur. Academy Award-winning actor, Denzel Washington, reinforced this same idea when he said, "Luck is where opportunity meets preparation."[2]

Put in the work with the necessary preparation, and opportunities happen. You just never know precisely when they will occur. It's the same concept for the understudy in a musical play. When a big break occurs as a fill-in for the star who can't perform, the understudy wows the crowd and launches a career. The point is simple. Are you willing to put yourself through the practice and conditioning to prepare for the opportunity? Those unwilling to do so miss out, and opportunities pass them by. That's a shame.

What would have happened at Cal State Fullerton if I was not dedicated to my trumpet practice? What would have happened if I had not invested all those hours in the practice rooms to improve my playing? Would Benton Minor have gone to bat for me with the administration? I'm glad I don't need to ponder those questions. I made good choices before presented with an opportunity disguised as a crisis. And those experiences simply prepare us for the real world.

Do you remember your first real job? If you're not there yet, expect a few memorable moments. Some will be positive, and some will not. Either way, powerful experiences with many lessons await you. And often, unexpected twists and turns create those unexpected opportunities. Prepare yourself. You may be asked to do some things that others may be unwilling to do. As long as they are ethical and in line with your Core Values, then give them your best shot. As Dr. Anonymous wisely said, "Successful people are willing to do what unsuccessful people are unwilling to do." How true that is!

My first corporate experience provides a good example. It started off much differently than expected and unlike anything I imagined or anticipated. In my interviews, the corporate office buzzed with noticeable activity. The company's high growth mode created energy. More than nine hundred people worked in the corporate office of this national restaurant chain. Parking spaces were at a premium. The two days of intensive interviews opened my eyes to a new world. I interviewed first for one position with some staffers. At the end of day two, I was hired me for a totally different position. I was selected to head up an unadvertised position as head of the corporate training department with sixty-seven people.

On day one, my new boss George and I met in the Philadelphia regional office. In his twenty-year career with the company, he had advanced to the Director of Human Resources Director and now reported to the Vice President of Personnel. I looked forward to working with George to learn from his wealth of knowledge and experience.

After brief meetings at the regional office, we visited field training stores to help me gain a better sense of the operations. Then, just two days into the trip, George received a phone call. When he hung up, he told me he immediately needed to return to corporate and for me to tour on my own. I didn't think much of it at the time.

The regional training directors and store managers helped me gain insight into my new world. As I worked alongside the management trainees, I picked up examples of the training materials and formulated ideas on how to improve what was already in place.

A week and a half later and on the plane flight back to corporate, I reviewed my notes and the materials collected. A man stopped right next to my aisle seat and said, "Bill?" My college band director, Benton Minor, was traveling home from a music educators' conference. A delightful conversation ensued, as we caught up on each others' lives.

Upon my return, I set off for my first day at corporate. As I drove into the parking lot, I noticed the availability of many open parking spaces. I thought, "Well it *is* Friday. There must be a lot of people traveling. Or maybe folks left early to stretch their weekends." I smiled as I imagined how corporate life might be.

As I walked into the reception area for George's office, his assistant, Catherine, had her head buried in her arms sobbing. She looked up at me with teary eyes and said, "George needs to see you right away. He's waiting in his office." On the phone, he motioned for me to sit down with a troubled look on his face. When he hung up, he brought me up to speed.

While we were away, a hostile takeover occurred. The

holding company installed a new senior management team. They terminated two-thirds of the corporate staff during the week. I thought, "Well that explains why it was so easy to find a parking space!" Then he dropped the bombshell. In a matter-of-fact tone George said, "Bill, everything's changed. I leave the company today. You now report directly to John, the VP of Personnel." He said that was it. As he started to pack his personal belongings, he said if I had any questions, it would be better for me to see John.

I left George's office and quickly headed down the hall right into John's office. I simply asked, "Is my job secure?" He assured me it was. He said the need for my skills was greater than ever. His response comforted me. I had developed a comfortable rapport with John a few weeks earlier in my final interview for the job. There had been no time for a real personal attachment to form between George and me.

Reassured, I focused my mental energy on the challenge ahead. Even with the trauma and turmoil, the opportunity to work at the headquarters of the largest restaurant chain in the country provided me with a growth framework. As John and I discussed the project I started, he told me to continue on with it. As we finished the conversation, I asked him where he wanted me to sit and get to work. After an uncomfortable blank stare, John quickly realized an omission. In all the confusion, no one set aside any office space for me.

As we left his office, we passed plenty of open offices in the long hallways. On the second floor, he found a small office and told me to take up temporary residence there. He encouraged me to settle in and left quickly. He had plenty of work to do.

I sat at my new desk and took a deep breath. As I collected my thoughts, I breathed out a big sigh. I uttered under my breath to no one in particular, "Boy, this wasn't exactly how I pictured my first day at corporate." I paused, shrugged my shoulders, and threw myself into the materials I collected during my trip. I reviewed some revisions already made on the flight home.

After just a minute of quiet focused time, a distinguished-looking gray-haired man in a pinstriped suit appeared at my door. He popped his head in my office door, stuck out his right hand and said, "Hi I'm Dan. I'm the president of the company. Who are you?" As I shook his hand, I replied, "I'm Bill Cole, the new training guy." A quizzical look crossed his face. He paused for a moment and said, "Oh, okay. Come see me in my office." And then he turned around and *whoosh* – he was gone.

I thought, "This is good. The president of the company wants to chat a bit, get acquainted, and welcome me to the company. That's nice!"

By the time I got out from behind my desk and out my office door, he disappeared. He was nowhere to be seen. I looked down the long corridor to my right and then down the equally long corridor on my left. At that precise moment, I realized that I didn't even know where the bathroom was yet, let alone where the office of the president might be. I simply guessed and turned left. As I briskly walked to the end of the corridor, I heard a voice to my right, so I turned there. Further down the corridor was a large corner office. The voice seemed to be coming from there, so that's where I headed.

As I approached the open door, it was impossible to avoid hearing, "That's the stupidest *!@*! most (blankety-blank) thing I've ever heard! You call yourself a VP? Well you stupid (blankety-blank *!@*!), you won't be for long." I reached the doorway just in time to see Dan, with his back to me, slam down the phone at his desk. It was surreal. In this beautifully appointed corner window office with a stunning view of the mountains, Dan turned towards a large man sitting on a couch. Dan's red face scarcely detracted from the veins bulging out from his neck. He looked right at the large man whose hands tightly gripping his knees. Dan then screamed something like, "Ed, that guy's an idiot. Whack him!"

At that moment, Dan saw me as I stood in the doorway. He motioned me in with his finger and pointed to the couch. I sat down next to Ed and leaned back. I hoped to calm things down a bit. After all, I looked forward to the chance to get acquainted. Dan looked right at me. He then screamed at the top of his lungs, "Where's your yellow pad? How can you do any work without a yellow pad? We need to get some work done around this (blankety-blank *!@*!) place!"

I immediately jumped off the couch and told him I'd be right back. I ran at full speed back down the two long corridors to my office to get a yellow pad. I rummaged through my desk that I barely opened before as I looked for a yellow pad. I thought, "Stay calm, Bill. These folks still put their pants on one leg at a time just like you do. You've faced tougher challenges than this."

I arrived back at Dan's office with my yellow pad in hand and out of breath. He again pointed me to the couch. As I sat down, he launched into a nonstop five minute lecture. He told me exactly how he wanted the management recruiting and training program to work. I wrote furiously on my yellow pad. Then he paused, took a depth breath, looked directly at me, and said, "Any questions?" I shook my head and said no. Dan said, "Go. Make it happen! We're done." I jumped off the couch, left his office, and headed back down the corridor. As I sat back down at my desk, I remember shaking a bit as I thought, "This *really* isn't how I pictured my first full day at corporate! I need to get on this right away."

Within twenty seconds, the phone rang. It was John. He wanted to see me in his office right away. So off again I went. At least I knew where his office was! As I went downstairs and arrived at John's office, he asked for an update. Without the graphic details, I described my five minutes of note-taking from the president on the new direction of the management recruiting and training program. John seemed surprised that Dan called me into his office. He knew nothing about the new direction.

After a slight pause, John asked if I was willing to put in some extra work with him over the weekend. He felt we needed to work together on this project. He wanted it completed and ready for his boss, Ed, first thing on Monday morning. Without hesitation I said, "Yes." I already anticipated the need to sacrifice much of the weekend to complete the project.

With hindsight and perspective, I believe the episode presented by John (or even Ed and Dan) may have been a test of my willingness to work. Did I have the character, thick skin, and work ethic necessary to survive in this new corporate culture? When I look back on that memorable first day and the extra work required, I now realize how it led to my next five years of opportunities.

How you react or respond to difficult challenges you most certainly will face determines the direction of your journey. Difficult circumstances often create unexpected opportunities, powerful learning experiences, and motivation. Within a few months, John left the restaurant chain for another opportunity. I then reported directly to Ed, the Executive Vice President. A numbers guy, he held the position of Chief Financial Officer. I learned a lot about finance from him. When they hired a new Senior Vice President of Operations, they assigned me to him. An expert in restaurant operations, Frank understood the value of training and development. He understood the importance of placing the right people in the right positions.

As we worked together and Frank saw me in action, his

level of respect grew for my skills. We recruited an entirely new regional staff. He saw first-hand how motivated people were when they worked with me. My knowledge of the restaurant industry and store operations increased dramatically. Even though this first corporate job turned out much differently than I imagined, I thrived on the challenge. What a great learning opportunity in the first phase of my corporate career!

My advice is not to overly anticipate what to expect when you get started in any new environment. It's unlikely to be all fun and games. Challenges will be involved. In my two years with the national restaurant chain, my former boss John stayed in touch with me. He accepted the position of VP of Personnel with a computer peripherals manufacturing company – the largest of its kind world-wide. The explosive growth in the computer industry created an atmosphere of fierce competition for talented personnel.

When the timing was right, I changed industries to apply my recruiting and training skills in this totally different environment. In my initial role, I developed a college internship program for engineers and business students, plus an on-campus recruiting program. With success in my first assignment, additional growth opportunities presented themselves for me to grow in other areas of human resources.

My next assignment led to my next opportunity. An engineering vice president headed the next generation research and development team. His charter was to start up a manufacturing division. This new product was viewed as the key to the company's future. I was appointed a divisional director of human resources reporting to the operational vice president with a dotted line back to John.

In my new role as a member of the division's leadership team, I designed and executed the recruitment strategy for the key executives. I developed innovative interview processes. We designed the entire physical layout of a new state-of-the-art manufacturing facility. I implemented training programs. I served as the plant employee relations liaison with corporate. As I gained exposure and hands-on experience in manufacturing, my growth accelerated.

After a corporate re-structure, John brought me back to his department as Corporate Recruiting and Training Director. Then he abruptly left the company. About the same time, one of my colleagues, an employee relations manager, submitted her resignation. Although many thought I would replace John, a surprise occurred. She was promoted into John's role. I now reported to her. Within days, she called me into her office and gave me the choice to resign or be fired. I chose to resign.

The trauma of a corporate power play is never fun. It was painful at the time. So pay close attention to what I'm about to say. As painful as the loss of a job can be, many people with a similar experience will tell you the same thing. It was the best thing that ever happened to me. It furthered my career. In fact, it catapulted me forward.

Here's what happened next. After a few days of recovery from the shock and self-pity, I called my business contacts for job leads. As a break, I called my brother Norm to wish him a happy birthday. He asked how things were going on my job. I briefed him on what had just happened. Coincidentally – although the truth is there are no coincidences – Norm just started a new business venture. He said that he thought it might be a good fit for me. Although I'd never really been that close to Norm growing up because of our age difference, I knew he built four successful businesses from the ground up. One had been the largest of its kind in the nation before he sold it. Early in his career, he was a successful sales professional.

But a small entrepreneurial company like Norm's was

not in my frame of reference. I was familiar with corporate America – not an entrepreneurial environment. I remember with embarrassing clarity saying: "Norm, if there's one thing that's true, I will *never... ever* work for or with you in business." And then I hung up.

Three weeks later, I assisted Norm in the start-up of his new business venture. I committed to move from Santa Barbara to Sacramento on a commission-only basis. He truly was a great salesperson! Of course, it's easy to be a great salesperson, with excitement and enthusiasm for what you do. Great salespeople also don't give up easily after they are initially told no.

In this start up business, Norm acquired franchises of a business development firm. The franchisor's marketing strategy targeted small business owners. A two and one-half hour seminar outlined what happens to most small business owners who start their own businesses. At that point in my career, I had never presented a seminar. Norm, however, did not focus on my lack of experience. He saw my talent and potential. He saw what I did have. He saw my significant experience in the design and development of training programs. He saw my teaching background. He saw my many years of experience performing on stage. He visualized my ability to do the seminars well. His confidence in me overcame any hesitation or doubts. He knew I could do it. That's why he kept after me, even after I initially turned him down.

Learning that first seminar was daunting. It required the memorization of a 197 page script word-for-word. In addition, choreography was involved to deliver a flawless presentation. This monumental challenge required an all-consuming dedicated effort for the next six weeks. I worked six days per week and invested many long hours with the script. Some were twenty-hour days.

Do you recall the story about the young man who stopped an elderly lady on the street in New York? He asked her, "Ma'am, how do I get to Carnegie Hall?" She paused and said simply, "Practice, practice, practice!"

Even though I didn't realize it then, good public speaking skills are extremely useful. If that's true, why do so many people avoid developing those skills? Is it because so many people are afraid of speaking in public? Are you aware that public speaking is the most common fear in America? Death is well down the list at number six. What most people don't know which holds second place. It's *dying* while *speaking*!

Unchecked, this strong fear forms excuses. Many never summon the courage to overcome it. The former first lady and wife of the 32nd U.S. President, Eleanor Roosevelt, gave us some great advice. She said, "We gain strength, and courage, and confidence by each experience in which we really stop to look fear in the face... we must do that which we think we cannot."[3]

I advise you to stop and look fear in the face. Be willing to take it on. Do you realize most fears are not facts? While the emotions of fear may be real, what we perceive as facts often are not. Most fears stem from how we interpret the facts or evidence.

Let's illustrate that with a story. Three soon-to-be fathers nervously wait on the couch outside the hospital delivery room corridor for their wives to deliver their babies. Suddenly the doors swing wide open. A young nurse smiles broadly and says, "I have good news for Mary's husband." One man smiles, raises his hand, and says, "That's me!" The nurse smiles and says, "Sir, I'm pleased to tell you you're a proud papa. Mary just delivered twins!"

The man looks surprised. He says, "Oh, I wasn't expecting that." Then after a moment, a smile forms on his face. He says, "You know, I guess that's fine. I work for the Minnesota

Twins, so that's very appropriate. Can I see Mary and the twins now?" He gets off the couch and follows the nurse through the doors and into the delivery room.

A half hour passes. The two remaining men wait expectantly. The doors of the delivery room corridor again swing wide open. The nurse looks more disheveled than before. She smiles weakly, looks at the two men on the couch and says, "Which one of you is Sally's husband?"

One man raises his hand. The nurse lets out a deep sigh and says, "Sir, we're all a little surprised, but I'm pleased to tell you that you're a proud papa as well. Sally just delivered triplets!"

The man looks shocked. His eyes widen. He starts hyperventilating. He says, "Triplets! Oh my! Are you sure? We weren't expecting that. We had no idea." Then he pauses, takes a few deep breaths and calms down a bit. Finally he smiles and says, "Nurse, that's okay. After all, I work for 3M. I guess triplets are appropriate for us. Can I see Sally and the triplets now?" He gets off the couch and follows the nurse into the delivery room corridor.

The man left on the couch begins fidgeting nervously as the time drags on. His toes start tapping. He drums his fingers on the side of the chair. He starts sweating and rubs the back of his neck. As he watches the clock on the waiting room wall, it seems to stand still. Finally, the doors of the delivery room corridor swing open one more time. The nurse looks totally frazzled. She looks at him and before she opens her mouth, the man leaps off the couch and takes off running down the corridor in the opposite direction. The nurse chases after him. She yells out, "Sir, stop. I have great news for you!" Without breaking stride, he screams back, "Lady, I don't want to hear it. I work for 7-UP!"

Now that's fear. What's yours? Are the facts true, or is there false evidence appearing real? What we imagine the fear to be is often more real than the actual evidence associated with the fear. But imagined fears often drive us to actions that may not help us get to where we want to go.

Even though I practiced my seminar for hours on end, many moments of doubt occurred. Some days, I couldn't remember what I learned the previous day. How discouraging! Many fears blocked my progress with so many things to learn in the process. It was hard work. Sometimes, it didn't seem to be worth the effort. At times, I felt like giving up. But that never was a serious option. People counted on me. My obligation to them was as strong as it was to Norm. And the date of the first seminar loomed ahead with an entire team of people in place.

My wife Kristy supported me greatly. She monitored the script as I recited it from memory. She encouraged me. She believed I could do it. Two professional speech coaches gave me feedback and encouraged me. But the greatest lesson learned during this experience is also a key factor that so many successful people have discovered. This principle was perhaps best articulated by another American industrial giant of his era, John D. Rockefeller. He said, "I do not think that there is any other quality so essential to success of any kind as the quality of perseverance. It overcomes almost everything, even nature."[4]

Perseverance gets you through tough times and doubts. That was a key building block for me. Perseverance keeps you focused on the end result. Most of us have talents to produce extraordinary results already inside us. The key is to align our talents and interests with something we really want to do. Another key is to draw upon our strengths and use what's already at our disposal in a focused way. As the deadline loomed, I couldn't imagine another choice but to tough it out and persevere. The 6th U.S. President, John Quincy Adams, put it this way: "Patience and perseverance have a magical effect, before which difficulties disappear and obstacles vanish."[5]

At first, I followed someone else's prescribed approach to learn the seminar, and it wasn't working for me. I knew the deadline was at risk. So in my difficulties, I examined my strengths. After all, when something doesn't work the way it should, it's time to try something else and be creative. I tapped into my performance background and applied a musical technique to memorize the script. My progress accelerated.

By the evening of the first seminar, I knew the seminar content and flow so well, that I could visualize the words in my head. Most professionals tell you that's a good sign for a professional actor or presenter. Due to my preparation, I internalized the script. Preparation gives you that advantage. I was also nervous. But nervousness properly focused gives you an edge. When it's show time, remember this quote from Dr. Norman Vincent Peale. He said, "The more you lose yourself in something bigger than yourself, the more energy you will have."[6]

As I started the seminar, hundreds of hours of preparation took over and the nervousness went away. My energy focused my delivery of the message and connected with the audience. No distractions caused me to search for the right words. No missed opportunities to connect with the audience occurred due to a lack of preparation.

It was the same when I took the game winning shot at Cal. No distractions from competing players or the fans got in the way. My mental and physical preparation conditioned me for that moment. I knew I could make that shot. I wasn't afraid to try.

My first seminar repeated that experience. I knew I could do it. Others believed in me and gave me the opportunity. I believed in myself. I did the work necessary to perform well.

My education and training background added a depth of knowledge, and I owned that seminar. I took full advantage of that opportunity.

Years later, I still remember the one short reminder sentence just before intermission that I left out. That was it... out of 197 scripted pages! The result was powerful. More Clients signed up for our services than from any other seminar before in the entire franchise network. That night confirmed a new professional calling!

Without the combined effect of hard work, practice, conditioning, perseverance and encouragement, the result would not have been achieved. Benton Minor conducted bands with that same principle. He often said when you rehearsed well, you perform well. Frank Poucher coached water polo the same way. Allan Trefry followed the same advice with his bands and orchestras. Norm Cole also applied it. Pablo Picasso, the famous twentieth-century painter, said, "Inspiration does exist, but it must find you working."[7]

In any field, lasting success happens not by accident or chance or luck. Music, athletics, academics, or any meaningful pursuit all require the willingness to work. As Zig Ziglar says, "The most beautiful philosophy in the world will not work if you won't. Success is dependent upon your glands, your sweat glands."[8]

This enduring Core Value of a willingness to work combined with confronting your fears and perseverance is a powerful combination. With encouragement from others, the opportunity to be a nearly un-stoppable force presents itself. When preparation and opportunity combine with talent and a willingness to learn, success happens.

You determine your level of achievement with your talents, your self-discipline, your willingness to work, your perseverance, plus your willingness to overcome your fears.

Focus on your capabilities and put forth the effort necessary to travel boldly on your journey. Let *The ABC Formula* spring to life and determine how far you go in your chosen path.

So where do you start? Begin right where you are, with what you do, and with what you have right now. Apply yourself with a dedicated work ethic. Make that choice today. Remember that it's not enough to sit in front of an empty fireplace and say, "Give me heat." Nothing happens until you do the necessary work to create the proper environment. For a roaring fire, first put in the chopped wood logs, the paper and kindling, and then light the match. Do the work first. It's always necessary, before you get the result.

No matter how smart you are, it matters more how well you apply the smarts you have. Remember this formula from one of the great inventors of all time, Thomas Edison. He said, "Genius is one percent inspiration and ninety-nine percent perspiration."[9] Be willing to put in the effort first.

Embrace the enduring Core Value of work and the other components of *The ABC Formula*. With them, you capitalize on your skills, talents, and abilities in whatever path you choose to follow. This key building block will always serve you well.

Be Willing to Do the Work Necessary
to Find Out the Truth.

Norman H. Cole

Chapter Eight Endnotes – Work

1. Bobby Knight. BrainyQuote.com, Xplore Inc, 2011. http://www.brainyquote.com/quotes/quotes/b/bobbyknigh122144.html, accessed January 3, 2011.
2. Denzel Washington. BrainyQuote.com, Xplore Inc, 2011. http://www.brainyquote.com/quotes/quotes/d/denzelwash377999.html, accessed January 3, 2011.
3. Eleanor Roosevelt. BrainyQuote.com, Xplore Inc, 2011. http://www.brainyquote.com/quotes/quotes/e/eleanorroo121157.html, accessed January 3, 2011
4. John D. Rockefeller. BrainyQuote.com, Xplore Inc, 2011. http://www.brainyquote.com/quotes/quotes/j/johndrock165071.html, accessed January 3, 2011.
5. John Quincy Adams. BrainyQuote.com, Xplore Inc, 2011. http://www.brainyquote.com/quotes/quotes/j/johnquincy387094.html, accessed January 3, 2011.
6. Norman Vincent Peale. BrainyQuote.com, Xplore Inc, 2011. http://www.brainyquote.com/quotes/quotes/n/normanvinc386105.html, accessed January 3, 2011.
7. Pablo Picasso. BrainyQuote.com, Xplore Inc, 2011. http://www.brainyquote.com/quotes/quotes/p/pablopicas378943.html, accessed January 3, 2011
8. Zig Ziglar, *The Attitude and Altitude Connection,* (Krestcom Productions, Inc., 2005 dvd)
9. Thomas A. Edison. BrainyQuote.com, Xplore Inc, 2011. http://www.brainyquote.com/quotes/quotes/t/thomasaed109928.html, accessed January 3, 2011

Truth

Half a truth is often a great lie.[1]
Benjamin Franklin, U.S. Statesman

P hilosophers throughout the ages studied these questions: "What is truth? How do we find out the truth?" This search continues today.

A successful search for the truth requires the enduring Core Value of hard work, but hard work, by itself, is not enough. We need direction to accomplish any desired result. With direction, hard work applies skills and knowledge to a given situation, resulting in wisdom. This building block enables us to find out the truth. And the truth – what's really there – comes not only from what is said and done on the surface of things, but also what lies beneath. It comes from understanding the beliefs and motivations that explain what we see and experience. This helps you discern and comprehend the full picture of what is really going on.

Let me share an example. At the beginning of my brother's new business venture, my public speaking skills grew rapidly through hard work and experience. After the two and a half hour marketing seminar, Norm assigned me to present twenty additional two-hour seminars. That challenged me! The topics of organization, management, and operations matched my previous experience. Others, like finance, marketing, and sales, stretched my comfort zone. With focused effort, practice, and experience, my competence grew as did my confidence. My growth in skills enabled me to fully engage my participants – or so I thought.

We all know that not everyone learns the same way, and many learn by asking questions. When someone asked a question, I initially answered without careful consideration of my response. Since I absorb information rapidly, I believed quick answers demonstrated my expertise. My ego contributed to this bad habit.

But I discovered another contributing factor – my discomfort with silence. Have you known people uncomfortable with silence? Sure. Is silence a bad thing? Not necessarily.

Listen to the compositions of such classical musicians as Beethoven and Mozart. They filled their music with dramatic pauses and silence. These effects add drama and draw attentiveness to what comes next. The old saying "Silence is golden" is good to remember. There are times when words do nothing but distract from beauty. Imagine a beautiful sunset or dramatic vista. The same truth applies in the context of a learning environment. Learn to embrace silence, particularly when the alternative is rambling conversation not easily connected to the topic at hand.

Early on, I had no real understanding of the value and power of silence as it applied in learning environments. Often, I filled in the silence after a question, while I searched inside my head for a good answer. That strongly ingrained habit bought me time. At least that's what I thought until a day when I was sitting in Norm's office, he asked me a question. To buy more thinking time, I rambled on. My long-winded discourse on related issues filled the room, while I formulated my answer.

At first, Norm patiently listened. Then he stopped me in mid-sentence. He said, "Bill, I swear you'll run out of *ideas* long before you run out of *words*." Like a ton of bricks, his comment stopped me dead in my tracks. With my full attention captured, he said, "It's not the quantity of what you say. It's the quality of what you say that counts. Less is more."

Norm taught me a key building block of effective communication right then. He broke my cycle and discomfort with silence. Now I realize how vitally important this skill is in all walks of life. It's a prerequisite to find out the truth.

Author Madelyn Burley-Allen said, "We spend forty percent of our time listening, thirty-five percent talking, sixteen percent reading and nine percent writing."[2] That's almost exactly the inverse amount of the time spent during school in those areas. I find that interesting. Listen effectively. It leads you to find out the truth.

Here's how Norm explained why this is so important. Most people operate at a surface level. Eager to get on to what's next, they readily accept the first answer to their questions. Norm believed a person's first response *rarely* answered the question. If that's the case, then a gap of understanding the whole picture occurs and causes a disservice for all parties involved.

Norm encouraged me to use this litmus test. When someone speaks, he advised me to silently ask, "Am I listening while waiting for an opportunity to speak, or am I listening to truly understand?" Wow! This takes hard work, practice, and commitment. It puts the responsibility on you to listen more to the other person.

As I grew in this skill, I learned to listen not only for the *content* of what's said but also for its *intent*. How else do we gain understanding of where the other person is coming from? To truly understand rarely occurs at a surface level.

Norm also advised, "Be willing to ask questions that make you uncomfortable. Ask enough questions until you know the truth." This advice flies in the face of our conditioning. Think back to when you asked your parents, "Why?" Your parents patiently answered, for the first two or three times, until they tired of it. Then they instructed you to stop asking. That conditioned us to stop or risk discomfort. Most of us simply never learned to effectively re-frame and re-state our questions.

Norm encouraged me to re-learn the skill of asking questions. He wanted me to signal my interest and care for the other person. He encouraged me to go beyond the surface where most people operate, and really get to know others.

This skill now fuels my curiosity with empathy. It helps me probe for a deeper understanding of what's meant, beyond what's said. I connect more deeply now with others and in more significant ways. That brings me closer to finding out the truth. This crucial building block will serve you and others well, as you engage people beyond the surface level to understand their perspectives.

A related, and all too common, bad habit is letting others off the hook by allowing them *not* to answer questions. If you don't care enough or don't want an answer, then don't ask the question. If you truly care enough to engage someone, then pursue the answer until you truly understand it. If a question is important enough to ask, it's also important to receive and understand the answer. When we show others how much we care, it moves us toward a deeper level of trust. More trust fosters more engagement. So be relentless to find the truth, and pursue it with positive intention.

The author Karl W. Palachuk is a colleague. He says, "The transition from talking to listening requires humility."[3] Although Norm's ego was strong, a spirit of humility exuded from him. It's something I strive for, but it's not easy to attain. A spirit of humility requires hard work. To be a good listener also requires hard work. But with both, you create opportunities to connect with, and more deeply understand others.

In our earlier discussion of the Core Value of honesty, we stressed the importance of being transparent. Transparency means *not* hiding the truth. But it also means you are open and willing to *tell* the truth. This concept tests many. But it's another vital building block, because it advances your ability to see the whole picture –both above and below the surface. I *know* your willingness to tell the truth helps your ability to find out the truth.

I mentioned earlier the old saying, "The truth hurts." But I disagree, if the intent is to help. If the purpose in telling the truth is to tear someone down, then the truth *will* hurt. In that case, it's better left unsaid. The difference is intent.

Here's a personal example. A few years ago, I met a regional manager for a large national company. He was bright and sincerely interested in what I offered. In our introductory meeting, we built an excellent rapport. He asked me to schedule another presentation with two of his support staff.

In my line of work, I meet and work with key executives who lead a variety of organizations. They tend to be very nice and sincere people. That's why they achieve a significant level of responsibility. The negative stereotype of executives pushing others out of the way or climbing over them is disturbingly exaggerated. People overwhelmingly get ahead in organizations, because they work hard and live by enduring Core Values. My entire career experience contains very few negative meetings.

Unfortunately, the second meeting with the regional manager's support staff was one of those negative experiences. I felt attacked for no apparent reason. One person treated me rudely. His colleague treated me with unprofessional indifference. Obviously, their unstated agenda undermined our meeting. It left a bad taste in my mouth.

In that situation, I could have simply walked away without another word. But I felt the better choice was to schedule another meeting with the regional manager. When we met, I asked him to share his people's perceptions of our meeting. He said they reported that I didn't have anything of value to offer. I asked for his permission to give him my perception of the meeting, and he said of course. Before I started, I explained that I thought it would be valuable for him to know my perspective and impressions as a potential vendor. I also made it very clear that in no way was I trying to tear down his people. Interestingly, my feedback wasn't unique. He had received similar comments on them before. He thanked me sincerely for my honesty and my willingness to tell him the truth.

My intent was to offer him a service, not for any other reason than to raise his awareness. I wanted to help him and his organization. It did not lead to any business with his organization. But my conviction demonstrated three enduring Core Values... service, honesty, and truth. And my intent was pure.

Another building block in the quest for the truth is the willingness and an eagerness to learn. It's much more than a goal. It's a lifelong pursuit that becomes a way of life. Benjamin Franklin said, "Being ignorant is not so much a shame, as being unwilling to learn."[4]

Opportunities to expand our knowledge abound, and you can learn through a variety of strategies and modes. Reading is a good start. In school, we're taught the key skill of reading. And yet, reading drops off dramatically in the general population after leaving school. The average adult reads only two books a year. If you're not reading to gain new information, you run the risk of stagnation. That can lead to developing a fixed perspective. Rather than lose the joy of growth, embrace the acquisition of more knowledge through reading.

Start by reading something good every day. John Wooden encouraged us to drink deeply from good books. Zig Ziglar advised us to read something good for twenty minutes per day. If we do that, we'll read the equivalent of twenty 200-page books each year. That's based on an average reading speed of 220 words per minute. Those additional eighteen books read per year gives you a significant advantage in knowledge and perspective.

The key is to advance your education through ongoing learning opportunities. Be committed to this ongoing process, whether it's through traditional books, e-books, trade magazines, podcasts, or other types of educational materials. Go to seminars and explore different areas of interest. Seek out information from a variety of sources. Discuss your interests with those more experienced than you are. Learn from every experience and everyone around you. As Abraham Lincoln said, "I do not think much of a man who is not wiser today than he was yesterday."[5]

This discovery path about yourself, the people around you, and the situations in which you find yourself can be both exhilarating and, at times, frustrating. Some people simply don't want to learn that much about themselves and others. They stopped learning when they finished school and ended their education. What about you?

With the rate of technological change, a typical college graduate's education is obsolete within five years of graduation. Futurist author Alvin Toffler says, "The illiterate of the twenty-first century will not be those who cannot read and write, but those who cannot learn, relearn, and unlearn."[6] For all of us, this means that the pursuit of education is ongoing. It's *not* a destination.

When people ask about my educational background, I often reply I have nine years of college and use very little of it today. Please avoid any misinterpretation of my point here. Higher education should be, and was for me, both a challenge and a wonderful experience. Everyone motivated to pursue it should do so and take advantage of every opportunity to learn in formal educational settings. Among many beneficial things, these experiences will help you to improve your thinking, your ability to research, and investigate information. They help your organizational skills, your approach to questions, your ability to deal more effectively with a wide diversity of people, and last but not least, your ability to survive a system.

Formal education serves an important and useful purpose in the lives of so many. It can be meaningful at any time in our lives and at any age. I love stories about people who return to academics in their later years to pursue an educational degree. A good example is Nola Ochs. In 2007 at the age of 95, she completed her degree in history at Fort Hays State University. She said, "Several years ago, I quit counting my age." What an inspiration for us all! She lived out this great advice from the author of *The Power of Positive Thinking*, Dr. Norman Vincent Peale. He said, "Live your life and forget your age."[7] Years ago, I heard Dr. Peale speak to his professional peers at an international conference. At the age of 92, he wowed us all as he demonstrated how an inspirational role model lives out his Core Values. What a privilege!

However, education is not always a straight-line experience. Kristy and I both had breaks in our formal schooling. Interestingly, both of us did significantly better in our academic pursuits after our respective breaks. Our experience is not unique. When people return to formal schooling after a break, they often return with a focused plan. They are motivated to accomplish what they set out to do. They apply themselves diligently to their goal. That was true for us.

When we went back to school, both Kristy and I more deeply understood the vital importance of *The ABC Formula* in our lives. We applied ourselves to achieve meaningful personal goals with a greater intensity of focus. You probably know others with similar experiences. We applaud their accomplishments. But that goal is not the sole reason for learning. Learning should not *just* be about the acquisition of knowledge. The goal is, and should be, to learn how to apply knowledge as we live our lives. A true educational process is as much about the journey as it is the destination. The older I get the more I discover what I don't know. How about you?

Let me challenge us all to answer these questions. What are we going to do about what we don't know? Will we pursue and apply ourselves to ongoing learning? Will we allow ourselves to be moved out of our comfort zones?

When you make positive choices and commit to ongoing learning, it creates opportunities to gain so much. Imagine what would happen if you embraced growth and pursued it vigorously. Would it...

✓ Improve your results in your chosen field?
✓ Improve your passion and purpose, and therefore your focus?
✓ Create more opportunities in your career?
✓ Improve your outlook on life?
✓ Positively impact your relationships?

The answer to all these questions is "Yes"! Make that

choice, and good things happen. With application of *The ABC Formula*, your results and relationships improve. Our results come from our pursuit of growth and how well we apply what we learn. Our world-view expands, which leads to further growth. And growth requires work.

I believe there are two phases of life: growth or decay. At all times, we're either in a growth or decay mode in some dimension in our lives. For me, I choose growth. What's your choice?

Through a commitment to ongoing learning, you acquire a greater depth of expertise, which in turn gives you greater insight in your areas of focus. Make a daily investment in yourself to improve and increase your knowledge. Strive to do this every day. This is a lifelong pursuit, not a temporary goal. Learn from your mistakes and avoid them next time. Understand the fundamental principle operating in any situation. Apply the principles that work in a given situation by analyzing the patterns that repeat from one environment to another. For some of us, it's a process that requires the ability to learn, unlearn, relearn and then learn some more. When you master the skill of learning how to apply knowledge to new situations, you gain wisdom. Seek the truth in all things.

I now understand more fully and deeply why Norm combined the willingness to work with the necessity to find out the truth as one enduring Core Value. The search for truth requires hard work. It requires the integration of many building blocks. That's why so many never find it. Take this to heart. Apply yourself to diligently search for the truth. A transformative effect is within your reach.

Be Willing to Do the Work Necessary
to Find Out the Truth.

Norman H. Cole

Chapter Nine Endnotes – Truth

1. Benjamin Franklin. BrainyQuote.com, Xplore Inc, 2011. http://www.brainyquote.com/quotes/quotes/b/benjaminfr141475.html, accessed January 4, 2011.
2. Madelyn Burley-Allen, *Listening: The Forgotten Skill* (NY: John Wiley & Sons, 1995) 2.
3. Karl W. Palachuk, *Relax Focus Succeed* (Sacramento, CA: Great Little Book Publishing Company, 2007), 138.
4. Benjamin Franklin. BrainyQuote.com, Xplore Inc, 2011. http://www.brainyquote.com/quotes/quotes/b/benjaminfr383680.html, accessed May 25, 2011.
5. Abraham Lincoln. BrainyQuote.com, Xplore Inc, 2011. http://www.brainyquote.com/quotes/quotes/a/abrahamlin101467.html, accessed May 25, 2011.
6. Alvin Toffler. http://www.alvintoffler.net/?fa=galleryquotes, accessed May 25, 2011.
7. Elizabeth Dole, *Hearts Touched with Fire: My 500 Favorite Inspirational Quotes* (NY: Caroll & Graf, 2004)

Initiative

Genius is initiative on fire.[1]
Holbrook Jackson, Author

Where does initiative come from? There may be as many answers to that question as there are different individuals. While initiative connects to many different parts of each one of us, initiative is most closely tied to motivation. So let's start there.

Are all people motivated? Certainly, we know people who are highly motivated and get a lot done. Then again, we know people who are lazy, disorganized, always late, and don't get much done. Are both groups motivated?

A few definitions of motivation give us insight to help answer this question. One source defines motivation as "the cause or reason why behavior occurs."[2] Another source defines it as "the reason for action."[3]

So the simple answer to the question – are both groups motivated? – is yes. When people are too lazy or disorganized to show up for work, to get to a meeting on time, or to attend a class, they are, in fact, motivated. They're simply more motivated to be lazy or disorganized than to be disciplined and on time!

So where does motivation come from? Another source defines motivation as the "forces acting either on or within a person to initiate behavior."[4] What this means is there are two different forces from which we draw our motivation. The first is the *within* forces – commonly called intrinsic motivators. The second is the forces acting *on* us – commonly called extrinsic motivators. More simply stated, we are motivated by either internal or external factors.

Think of it this way. In childhood, our parents or other authority figures rightly condition us to learn appropriate behaviors. Think of your experience as a child or student. You can just hear your parent or teacher say, "Hang on a minute. Don't do that yet! Wait until I tell you to." Those natural and simple examples of external factors or *extrinsic* motivation are, in most cases, not only appropriate but necessary.

As we grow and mature, we begin making more of our own choices of which behaviors to use in which situations. As those personal choices occur more often, we rely more and more on our own internal factors or *intrinsic* motivators. So our motivational patterns come from both internal and external factors. They are derived from our thoughts, personal experiences, the environments in which we've operated, and the conditioning we've been exposed to.

If you've been in situations that discourage independent action, then there's a good chance those situations discourage initiative. For example, a boss may have told you something when you first started work that paralleled a message from an early authority figure. You may have heard, "Hang on a minute. Don't do that yet! Wait until I tell you to." If this conditioning happens repeatedly (whether it's overt or subtle) and is left unchecked, it squelches initiative.

The result is the *indifference trap.* Some workers show up, do their job, and check out not only physically but mentally without offering suggestions for improvements. Some students get by with a minimum amount of effort far below their potential. Some volunteers participate in an activity without their talents and skills fully utilized and not challenged to give their best efforts. Some folks give in to peer-pressure and allow other activities to take priority over family plans. Some people show up for church, are entertained, have their felt needs met, and leave without commitment to spiritual growth. If factors like these are pervasive in an environment, then indifference reigns, and people shy away from initiative. The *tyranny routine* is the result.

Do you know people who work just for a paycheck and get no joy out of what they do? If you do, it's no surprise that many people don't even recognize opportunities and initiatives for what they are. Their strong conditioning causes them to wait for direction. They protect their comfort zones rather than expand them. They vigorously cling to and guard the status quo. They acquiesce to what Ronald Reagan observed, "Status quo, by the way, is Latin for the mess we're in."[5]

When people accept the status quo and cling to their comfort zones, a lack of motivation prevails. New ideas, initiatives, and changes in attitude are perceived as threats and resisted. The past is mentioned with reverence, as if it was the best part of their lives. We hear phrases like, "Remember how it used to be? Those were the good ole' days!" Rather than gaining twenty years of experience, they repeat one year's experience twenty times.

That's when the *apathy curse* begins. I offer no apologies for this strong term. Apathy means without passion. Unfortunately, apathy rules in too many environments and stifles growth opportunities – whether in families, in school, on a sports team, at work, in communities, or in churches. If you come to a standstill in your work, career, business, or any other path, keep in mind your competition is still moving forward. If you're not giving your best effort in school or on a team, your competitors will be giving theirs. If a church isn't deepening its members spiritually, they will look elsewhere.

When this conditioning is prevalent and pervasive in an environment, people are risk-averse or even risk-intolerant. They sadly fear the unknown. Over time, this conditioning breeds pessimism and negativity. When pessimism and negativity prevail, they stifle initiative.

This *apathy curse* is caused by a lack of initiative and motivation. It is an unfortunate by-product of this cycle. This unpleasant downward spiral sucks people into ruts. A friend and retired pastor, Dr. G. Henry Wells, once said that a rut is a grave with both ends open. Are there any ruts in your life right now?

If you are caught anywhere in this cycle, ask yourself what you need to do to overcome the *status quo*, the *tyranny routine,* or the *apathy curse.* Pull yourself out of your comfort zone. Avoid getting stuck in ruts. Avoid self-limiting thoughts and behavior that inhibit your potential to take the initiative to seize opportunities. Use *The ABC Formula* to support, foster, and reinforce forward movement for yourself and others. Develop and reinforce the habit to look for opportunities for growth.

Let me share a few examples from my own childhood. At the age of eight, I yearned to play guitar. I don't remember why, but it was *my* idea. I asked Mom. With Dad's permission, she signed me up for guitar lessons at the local music store. Robert Bennett was a fine musician and teacher. I made rapid progress with the support of my parents.

Mom was musical and had a fine voice. She sang at home, usually while baking and cooking. When I later discovered an old high school musical cast picture, she revealed that she had the lead in the production as a sophomore at Downey High School. Dad was not musical at all. In fact, he was tone-deaf – unable to distinguish pitches that were higher or lower. Even though music was not his talent, he supported my efforts completely. He attended my performances, conveyed enjoyment, and showed enthusiasm.

At the age of nine, I participated in a music class combined from several elementary schools. It was taught by Max Cutler, the junior high school music teacher. Max was a fine musician and teacher. Right away, he noticed my note-reading ability and sense of rhythm. Impressed, he approached Mom and learned I was studying guitar. Excitedly, he told Mom that he needed a guitar player for the junior high dance band. In no way was he deterred by the fact that I was three grades away from starting junior high. That was not an obstacle to him or a reason to avoid doing something. He auditioned me, and I joined the group. Mom shuttled me back and forth to rehearsals from the elementary school – right around the corner from home – to the junior high school a couple of miles away. She willingly made the extra driving trips. That experience jump-started my lifelong love of music.

Soon afterwards, I yearned to play the clarinet. I don't recall why. But I do remember another conversation with Mom. She skillfully directed me to the trumpet instead. My brother abandoned one that was stored on our closet shelf, when he was fitted with braces. I'm sure Dad's practicality came into play. I accepted the substitution of trumpet for clarinet with one condition – private trumpet lessons in addition to guitar. That was an early indicator of my budding negotiation skills. Max Cutler recommended a former student, Jay Daversa, to be my trumpet teacher. When I was nine and with Dad's consent, Mom signed me up for lessons with Jay,

Exceptionally talented, Jay was the top trumpet player at Whittier High School. At the ripe old age of fourteen, he performed professionally on a weekly Los Angeles TV show *Dixieland Small Fry*. Immediately, Jay's fine teaching impacted my playing. He focused my practice to develop my talent. As Max Cutler heard my consistent improvement, he initiated another conversation with Mom. He wanted me to play trumpet in the concert band at the junior high as a sixth grader. I was already a part of the musical scene at the junior high as the guitarist with the dance band. When I joined the concert band, Mom increased her chauffeur trips to at least three days a week for music rehearsals and performances.

By far the youngest kid, I started as the last chair of eleven trumpet players. After rehearsals every two weeks or so, Max held auditions. After each audition, I moved up one chair. Competition seemed natural to me – even at that young age. It must have come from playing cribbage and other games with Dad and my brother! I never considered age a limitation. Before long, I sat in the second chair in the trumpet section. As I look back, I'm amazed the older boys never took me out back to teach me a painful lesson. In fact years later, Mom told me that she and Max Cutler made a pact to prevent that from happening.

At the same time, Mom took piano lessons in a class of adults from Harold Graham. Harold was also a fine musician and great teacher. I enjoyed Mom's piano playing and her singing as she practiced. Then I initiated another conversation with Mom. It seemed quite natural to me, that I should also learn to play piano. Mom gained Dad's support, and I started private piano lessons with Harold Graham. At the age of eleven, I took three private music lessons every week. Even today, I'm amazed at the commitment made by my middle-class parents.

Since I was already an early riser, practice on one of my instruments started at 5:45 a.m. on most mornings before eating breakfast. In one way, it was hard work to practice scales and exercises plus learn new pieces. But in another way, music was like play. And there were rewards. The initial reward was simply improvement. Then the enjoyment of making good music became another reward in itself. Then the approval of others was another reward. Soon the practice and performing paid off in other ways. I played trumpet in a public performance with a small orchestra. I vividly remember receiving a $5 bill which I didn't expect. It was my first paid gig at the age of eleven! It was a revelation for me to find out that people would pay me to do what I loved doing.

At age twelve, five friends and I formed a musical combo – the Nocturnes. My best friend, Tom Hill, was the trombonist. Both of us were first chair players in the junior high concert band as seventh graders. Our drummer was Charles Drury, the pianist was Tom Silk, on tenor sax was Clark Sorenson, and on alto saxophone was Ken 'Dusty' Heller. We practiced several hours every week and our *'sound'* developed. Our talent, friendship, and love of playing were winning combinations. We relished the challenge of perfecting new songs. We gained satisfaction through hard work and play.

At the same time, Mom and Dad participated in ballroom dance classes from their friends, Jack and Doris Rogers. Doris was a particularly fine teacher and choreographer. One day, she shared her vision with Mom to form an exhibition ballroom dance group of youngsters. My name came up. In my early years, I studied ballet and tap dancing briefly. Mom asked me if I'd be interested in ballroom dancing. I said yes.

Although it was awkward at first to learn the dance routines, my sense of rhythm and music transferred well to dancing. My partner, Doris's daughter Penny, and I worked hard. We developed rapidly to become quite good. I loved performing.

Soon dancing and music created other opportunities.

Doris Rogers taught ballroom dancing in the area junior high schools. When the formal dance season came, our musical combo became the group of choice. Those junior high dance gigs led to other opportunities. As the parents who chaperoned the dances heard us, they recruited us to play for their adult dances. On many Saturday nights at the local country clubs, the Nocturnes played four hours of dance tunes while the adults danced to the music played by us young teenagers. We played consistently, developed a good reputation, and a loyal following. The money was a great reward as well.

During eighth grade, Max Cutler asked me to handle overflow trumpet students that Jay Daversa couldn't fill. At the tender age of thirteen, I became a bona fide music teacher. When Jay graduated from high school the following year, I picked up the slack from the void created when he enlisted in the Army Band. By the way, Jay was the first person to ever ace the Army's musical sight reading test with a perfect score.

By the age of fourteen, I engaged in a series of musical enterprises including performing and teaching. My teachers guided, nurtured, supported, and reinforced my efforts and talents. I consistently earned good money doing things I loved to do. None of it ever felt like work.

There are many building blocks to learn from here. When we're encouraged to act, initiative flourishes. Driven by initiative and the willingness to work, my entrepreneurial spirit was unleashed. But it did not happen in a vacuum. Look at all the people involved in these initiatives: myself, Mom, Dad, Robert Bennett, Max Cutler, Jay Daversa, Harold Graham, and Doris Rogers. True collaborations emerged. My parents and teachers identified, nurtured, shaped, and focused my talents. Without their support, my talent would have never developed as it did. But talent is only potential. While initiative often springs from talent, it must be nurtured by others. If anyone had not done their part, my musical talents would never have blossomed the way they did.

Initiative begins when you're encouraged to try something new, or when you take an extra step on your own without being directed by someone else. Parents dream of this for their children. Teachers look for this in their students. Employers dream of this with their employees. It's valued in all walks of life. Look for opportunities to identify moments that nurture and draw out the enduring Core Value of initiative in others. Encourage initiative rather than discourage it. With encouragement and support, we create opportunities to bear good fruit. An entrepreneurial spirit flourishes within this type of environment.

Think of the benefits when initiative is an enduring Core Value. Initiative shapes not only each one of us, but also the environment in which we live. I once heard that the greatest society is one composed of the greatest number of entrepreneurs. Our nation was founded and built by entrepreneurs – independent people who overcame obstacles. They focused on a vision of building a better future. Based on a culture of optimism, this entrepreneurial spirit imparted a willingness to try new things and take risks. It was imbedded into the fabric of our nation.

A culture based on initiative breeds innovation. Innovation drives entrepreneurial cultures. When this type of an environment is encouraged, talent is nurtured and becomes more visible. It's reinforced and recognized. This broadens the positive behavior patterns. A positive environment emerges. This is a very significant point.

We started with a discussion of motivation. Motivation

takes you only so far. When talent is identified and nurtured in ways that can be practiced and reinforced properly, motivation is focused. With focused motivation, practice, experience, and further reinforcement, these patterns develop into habits. Habits condition you to perform at higher levels. They are derived from the strength of our positive attitude about we do.

As we become more confident in our ability to apply our talents, our self-confidence grows. Our belief in our capabilities strengthens, and ultimately forms our convictions about what we do. With the talent level we have, this process of building new habits draws out our capabilities to reach our full potential. Then our habits become the outward reflection of our inner selves.

As you apply *The ABC Formula* more and more, it embeds itself into the fabric of your life. It's what spurs your growth. This enduring Core Value of initiative builds upon the foundation of the other enduring Core Values and carries over into all aspects of your life.

While ultimately productive and valuable, this process of growth is likely to be painful. This old saying – no pain, no gain – is so true. Growth requires a willingness to try new things, stretch, and learn. It is often necessary to break out of old non-productive habits and form new productive ones. We must be willing to break out of the status quo and take the initiative.

In my work, organizational executives consistently tell me they *long* for people with these values – people who are self-motivated and driven by intrinsic motivators. They know these people take the initiative with opportunities and take ownership to find solutions when challenges occur, even in the midst of disappointments.

The fact is there will always be some dark clouds on the horizon. But successful people develop the uncanny ability to peer through those clouds and see silver linings and possibilities. If you look long and hard enough at most situations, there is some good to be seen. There may be pain involved at the time, but if you keep trying, you will eventually see the good. I encourage you to look for the good in all things, even when it's difficult to do. It's the ultimate test of approaching all things with a positive attitude.

When we embrace this approach, our days fill with adventure. We search for opportunities to grow and make things better. When you choose growth, you operate by this building block stated so well by W. Clement Stone: "There is little difference in people, but that little difference makes a big difference. The little difference is attitude. The big difference is whether it is positive or negative."[6]

It's so true! The big difference of a positive attitude as you approach things helps you work on all the little things that make such a big difference. With it, homes run more smoothly. Relationships improve as they're worked on. Jobs work better with new innovations. New technology, tools, and processes improve our lives. During a musical performance, a small nuanced interpretation illuminates the composer's intent in new relevant and special ways. An actor's certain expression or articulation of a line evokes a strong emotion. Small incremental changes lead to large compounded effects. When we take responsibility to initiate and make small improvements in what we do, things change for the better. The willingness to take the initiative makes it happen.

For many, the natural tendency is just the opposite, due to so much conditioning in our respective environments that protects the status quo. Remember that there will be times when you'll need to encourage yourself and others to realize that it's acceptable to try something new. One good friend just started taking piano lessons at the age of fifty. I think that's terrific. If not now, when? That's always a good question to ask. Take the initiative. Try something new. It's never too late to stretch yourself. Sometimes it will change your life.

Here's my example. When I completed my double master's music degree, my goal changed from teaching in high school to teaching in college. My faculty advisors encouraged me to work on a doctoral degree, preferably on the East Coast to broaden my perspective and supplement my West Coast studies. As I searched for the right opportunity, I noticed a posting for a graduate assistantship to be the graduate assistant to the Director of Bands at Syracuse University in New York. That position called out to me. I felt *that* might be the ticket to accomplish my goal.

Without telling my bride of less than two years, I sent in my application. That's something I'm not proud of today. I feared Kristy would not be happy moving so far away from the rest of her family. Five months earlier and right after graduation with her Bachelor of Arts Degree in Accounting, she landed her dream job. She worked in the international accounting department at the corporate headquarters of the Union Oil Company in downtown Los Angeles.

A few evenings later when I was away at a rehearsal, Kristy received a call from the Director of Bands at Syracuse University. With an icy tone in her voice, she relayed the phone message to me. I fully understood why. When the band director and I connected later by phone, he offered me the position sight unseen. At the time, I was a faculty member for the Summer Music Academy at Cal State Fullerton. Dr. Frederick Fennell, the world renowned conductor of the Eastman School of Music Wind Ensemble in Rochester, New York not far from Syracuse, was the academy's guest conductor. The next day, I pulled Fred aside and asked for his opinion about my opportunity. He recommended without hesitation that I go to Syracuse.

When I told Kristy about the opportunity, she simply said, "Fine, go without me." Now I faced a real dilemma. I believed this opportunity was exactly the right step for my education and career. But I certainly was not going to jeopardize our relationship and young marriage. It didn't take too long for me to figure out what to do. This new initiative and opportunity would require more than just my own negotiating skills to overcome my wife's resistance. So I enlisted the aid of the one person she loved as much as me, her dad.

I called Bob Niemann, explained the situation, and he understood what this opportunity meant for me. I asked him to talk with his daughter. At the time, he also worked in downtown Los Angeles. Bob invited her to lunch. Before the meal, he ordered her a drink. Kristy never drank with her father before. She feared the worst and thought something must be terribly wrong. She thought to herself many times throughout the lunch, "What's wrong? Is Dad going to tell me that he's dying?" Finally, the small talk waned. At the end of the lunch, Bob simply said, "You should support your husband and go with him to New York." She hesitated slightly. She heaved a sigh of a great internal relief, because it wasn't the bad news she feared. She said, "Okay, I will."

The move to mid-state New York for two Southern Californians required a major adjustment in our early married years. We never knew that much humidity, changeable weather, rain, and snow existed. We left behind our circle of friends and family. In spite of the difficulties and in hindsight, everyone believes it was absolutely the right thing for us to do, both from a career stance, and from a personal one as well. We relied more on each other. We became more interdependent. It strengthened our marriage. The debt of gratitude I owe to Kristy's father is enormous. Thank you, Dad.

During my first semester at Syracuse, I played solo trumpet with a church choir directed by a music professor, Dr. Paul Eickmann. At the beginning of the rehearsal, I played a fanfare. Paul glanced at me with a pleased expression on his face and with a twinkle in his eyes. An instant connection formed. After the performance, Paul said I performed beautifully. He also said it was among the best trumpet playing he'd heard in Syracuse. That was a great encouragement. He asked me to play several more times at his church. I enjoyed the experiences and respected him as a musician. I thought it was interesting that he wasn't teaching courses in music even though he held a music faculty position. In the spring, Kristy and I accompanied Paul and the choir on a tour throughout New York and New Jersey. Our relationship grew based on our common musical bond and mutual respect.

As I had during my master's degree studies, I applied myself to my doctoral studies and earned straight A's. But I wasn't fulfilled. Something was missing. The rate of my musical development stagnated. I knew I needed something more, but I didn't know what. I searched for other course offerings. A new course caught my eye. The title *The Design, Development, and Evaluation of Instruction* intrigued me. Offered in the School of Education's Instructional Technology Department, I signed up for this second semester class.

In this class, a new world unfolded. During one memorable library study day, I reviewed some unpublished works suggested by the teachers. A paper on the topic of instructional development caught my attention. It laid out a systems approach to the improvement of undergraduate instruction. The educational formula concepts captivated me. I searched for the author. I saw a music professor authored the well-written article! It was by... (gasp!)... Dr. Paul Eickmann.

His paper inspired me. Immediately, my horizons broadened. I threw my heart into that course. My final paper analyzed several interesting inverse correlations between the improvement of teaching and tenure. My professors recognized the paper as outstanding. I received the top grade in the course.

But I wanted more. I thirsted to learn more about this fascinating subject – a new world to me. Near the end of the semester, I called Paul. I told him how much inspiration his paper gave me. I asked him to guide me in an independent study. We set an appointment to meet in his office at the Center for Instructional Development (CID).

When I arrived, Paul explained the mission of CID: "To improve the quality of undergraduate instruction at Syracuse University." The faculty and staff assembled at CID were dedicated to supporting other faculty to improve the quality of their teaching, courses, and curriculum. My imagination was captured with that compelling vision.

Has that ever happened to you? Immediately, something powerful unleashed from inside me. What happened to me at that moment may have been best described by Oliver Wendell Holmes: "One's mind, once stretched by a new idea, never regains its original dimension."[7]

At the end of our meeting, Paul said he'd be pleased to guide my independent study. He asked me to get back with him again in a couple of weeks.

When we met again, Paul introduced me to Assistant Vice Chancellor, Dr. Robert Diamond. Bob headed CID. As we chatted in his office, we quickly discovered a common bond. We both swam competitively in college in our respective eras. We immediately connected. It's really a small world, isn't it?

After a series of discussions with other staff throughout the day, Paul and I again met in his office. He offered me another opportunity. He proposed I switch my music department graduate assistantship to work with him as an instructional development intern at CID. That shocked me. I didn't know much about the subject and profession, much less how to apply it. But I *was* intrigued. An opportunity to do something I didn't even know existed just three months earlier was just presented to me. I asked Paul for time to think it through.

For two weeks, I agonized over the ramifications of the switch in my educational focus from music to something new. Never, in my wildest dreams, had I ever considered such a thought. Music was what I did and who I was. I'd spent a lifetime honing my skills. It was my comfort zone. My internal debate raged over the issues associated with what was comfortable – music – and what was unknown – instructional development. The difficult process challenged me.

Have you ever wrestled with a difficult choice? Most of us have. Sadly, many people never venture outside their comfort zone. They fear the unknown and stay where they feel safe. They operate in a world described by Nido Qubein: "People would rather be comfortable than be excellent."[8]

Dr. Eickmann recognized talents in me that I didn't see. Sometimes that's how life is. Others often see things you don't. His broader world view provided insight I didn't have. And yet the magnitude of this change overwhelmed me. There were pros and cons to consider. Finally, I realized that if I didn't take advantage of this opportunity, I would never *know* if it was right for me. I knew I could always go back to music if it didn't work out. But I truly felt that if I didn't try this, then one day I'd face the possibility of looking back with regret. I decided to go for it.

When you take initiative, new vistas open for you to explore. But it's up to you to take the first step. You must seize the moment to capitalize on the opportunity. You must take the initiative. No one can do it for you.

Stop for a moment. Look up and around. Many opportunities are there to be found. It's your responsibility to seek them out and find something that excites you. When you're excited about what you do, it's easy to be fulfilled. Hard work is so much easier when you tap into a passionate source of powerful energy. You approach things in a way similar to one of the most famous entrepreneurs, P.T. Barnum, who created joy for millions with his circus. He said, "Whatever you do, do it with all your might. Work at it, early and late, in season and out of season, not leaving a stone unturned, and never deferring for a single hour that which can be done just as well as now."[9]

This is good advice. Be willing to take the initiative. Look for opportunities to stretch and grow. Overcome any negative imprints and conditioning that may have been imposed from your background or environment. In our changing world, staying in your comfort zone is simply unacceptable.

Think outside your zone of defined limitations. The great American industrialist, Henry Ford, once said, "Whether you think you can, or that you can't, you are usually right."[10] In order to achieve something, you must first think it's possible. When I started work with Paul, I didn't really know what instructional development was. But my imagination was captured. Inspiration propelled me into action. As Brendan Francis Behan, an Irish playwright said, "Inspirations never go in for long engagements. They demand immediate marriage to action."[11]

In my new environment, my first assignment beckoned. I participated in the Retreat on Instructional Development. Sponsored by CID, this retreat was held at the Sagamore Institute in the beautiful Adirondack Mountains without outside interference from television on the conference grounds. Paul wanted me to observe and learn, while I mingled with professionals in the field. This particular conference was held during the Summer Olympics Games. Since the days were filled with intensive meetings, people wanted updates on the Olympics. So Paul presented me with another unusual opportunity. Both Paul and Bob Diamond knew of my Junior Olympic swimming championship background, so they asked me to provide Olympic update reports during meal times. I eagerly accepted.

In my free time, I scoured newspapers. I gathered not only sports results but also selected unusual stories to supplement my reports. I used the reports to have some fun as I presented the information. My mini Olympic meal reports highlighted the conference. I received great exposure to top professionals in the field. This wonderful platform provided me with a quick way to get to know other participants better. That simple initiative was an opportunity seized. You never know precisely when you'll get an opportunity. When it does present itself, take the initiative and seize the moment.

The rest of the conference enlightened me. I absorbed information and learned from top educational professionals, as they shared best practices in my new field. After the conference, I applied myself vigorously to my new role as CID Instructional Development Intern.

Paul guided my initial consultations with faculty members eager to improve their instruction. For my first project, I collaborated with a math professor, Danny Hakim. He taught a remedial program for freshman to help them catch up on basic math skills. Together, we developed a series of programmed instruction booklets which won a state award. In my second project, I worked with Cathy Rogers, a professor who taught a course on human sexuality.

Under Paul's direction, my lack of academic expertise in a faculty member's discipline became a strength and not a weakness. While the faculty member focused on the content, I challenged the presentation and methodology of instruction. When appropriate, I recommended technology-enhancements to increase students' understanding and retention of the classroom content. The course evaluations and student feedback guided redesign enhancements to maximize effectiveness of the learning environment.

This new work captivated me. Inspired to learn more, I studied books, articles, and unpublished papers on the subject. I absorbed all the information I could. I interviewed faculty, other staff members, and experts in the field. Paul's wonderful mentorship encouraged my zillions of questions. Carefully and patiently, he guided my development. My new calling led me to become a valued resource advisor to the faculty at Syracuse University. I was excited and passionate about my new field.

The ABC Formula was at work inside me. What started out as a positive attitude developed into a strong belief about my new field, which convicted me to give my best effort. Paul and I grew closer.

A few months later on a cold wintry day, Paul invited me to accompany him on a consulting assignment. As we drove on the New York State Thruway, he disclosed he received a new job offer. It was an overseas assignment to teach instructional development for the Educational Radio and Television Network in Teheran, Iran. The first responsibility was to develop the six month course curriculum. Then, Paul was to teach masters' degree students how to do what we did at Syracuse. The objective was to train instructional developers. The overall mission was to help the country educate its people and pull itself into the twentieth century. The best and fastest way to do this was to reach remote outlying areas with undeveloped school systems by satellite broadcasts of educational radio and television programs. The head of the national network reported to the Shah of

Iran, one of the most powerful men in the world at the time. As Paul described the opportunity, my excitement bubbled over with enthusiasm. Although I had mixed feelings about losing his mentorship, this incredible opportunity matched perfectly with his skills. I told him he needed to go. This cross-cultural project could have a large impact on people's lives on a grand scale. He agreed – it was a fabulous opportunity.

Two weeks later in his office, Paul told me he turned the job down. With his wife and three young girls as well as his university commitments, he felt the timing wasn't right. I expressed my disappointment, but I understood his reasons for not taking it. Paul then said he recommended someone else for the job. I asked him who. As he looked at me carefully, he paused. Then he quietly said, "Bill, I recommended you for the job." Flabbergasted and speechless, I just stared at him with wide-open eyes.

Think about this situation for a moment. Would this opportunity have presented itself, if I hadn't taken the earlier initiatives, explored something new, and reached deep inside myself to learn all I could? No. This opportunity resulted from a series of initiatives that placed me there at this precise moment.

When unleashed, initiative focuses our level of motivation and creates opportunities. It's not about luck or circumstances. The author of *As a Man Thinketh*, James Allen, insightfully said, "Circumstances do not make the man, they reveal him."[12]

With initiative, your mental focus becomes a powerful ally. It's been said that if you're capable of formulating a specific goal or conceiving something in your mind, the potential already exists within you to achieve it. My experience validates this. So does the experience of others I coach. Walt

Disney also spoke of this from his personal experience. He said, "If you can dream it, you can do it."[13]

Resist the temptation to underestimate your own potential and capabilities. Limit your fear. Pursue opportunities vigorously and follow your dreams. When you feel yourself about to hold back, move ahead. Take the initiative to try something new. Remember what the respected author, George Eliot said, "It is never too late to become what you might have been."[14]

After I discussed the Iran opportunity with Kristy, we collectively said, "Yes, we'll go!" Today, we often joke about how much easier it was to move from Syracuse, New York to Teheran, Iran than it was to move from Los Angeles to Syracuse! This unprecedented experience so early in our careers living in a foreign culture, traveling internationally, and broadening our horizons grew us both professionally and personally.

When captivated and excited by initiative, *The ABC Formula* unleashes a powerful force of internal motivation. This enduring Core Value allows you to accomplish more than you ever thought possible.

Take the Initiative.

Norman H. Cole

Chapter Ten Endnotes – Initiative

1. Holbrook Jackson. BrainyQuote.com, Xplore Inc, 2011. http://www.brainyquote.com/quotes/quotes/h/holbrookja380089.html, accessed January 4, 2011.
2. Westmont College, Department of Psychology. www.elitewellness.com/definition-of-motivation.html, accessed July 27, 2011.
3. www.wordreference.com, http://www.wordreference.com/definition/motivation, accessed July 27, 2011.
4. Britannia Encyclopedia, http://www.britannica.com/EBchecked/topic/394212/motivation, accessed July 27, 2011.
5. Ronald Reagan. BrainyQuote.com, Xplore Inc, 2011. http://www.brainyquote.com/quotes/quotes/r/ronaldreag183973.html, accessed January 4, 2011.
6. W. Clement Stone. BrainyQuote.com, Xplore Inc, 2011. http://www.brainyquote.com/quotes/quotes/w/wclements193770.html, accessed January 4, 2011.
7. Oliver Wendell Holmes. BrainyQuote.com, Xplore Inc, 2011. http://www.brainyquote.com/quotes/quotes/o/oliverwend161303.html, accessed January 5, 2011.
8. Nido Qubein. *Coping with Change: Strategies for Excellence* (Krestcom Productions, Inc., 1994 video)
9. P. T. Barnum. BrainyQuote.com, Xplore Inc, 2011. http://www.brainyquote.com/quotes/quotes/p/ptbarnum163291.html, accessed January 5, 2011.
10. Henry Ford. BrainyQuote.com, Xplore Inc, 2011. http://www.brainyquote.com/quotes/quotes/h/henryford131621.html, accessed January 4, 2011.
11. Brendan Francis. BrainyQuote.com, Xplore Inc, 2011. http://www.brainyquote.com/quotes/quotes/b/brendanfra104945.html, accessed January 5, 2011.
12. James Allen. BrainyQuote.com, Xplore Inc, 2011. http://www.brainyquote.com/quotes/quotes/j/jamesallen148444.html, accessed January 5, 2011.
13. Walt Disney. BrainyQuote.com, Xplore Inc, 2011. http://www.brainyquote.com/quotes/quotes/w/waltdisney130027.html, accessed January 5, 2011.

14. George Eliot. BrainyQuote.com, Xplore Inc, 2011. http://www.brainyquote.com/quotes/quotes/g/georgeelio161679.html, accessed January 5, 2011.

Accountability

Life is not accountable to us.
We are accountable to life.[1]
Dr. Denis Waitley, Author

Norm Cole used the word accountability frequently. When I wrote it on the list of his Core Values, it jumped off the page for me.

So let's define accountability. Accountability often relates to areas of governance. Business usually connects it to responsibility. In either case, it implies an expectation of account-giving to someone else. In fact, the root definition of accountability means *to stand up and be counted.* In earlier times, people voted this way.

When you stand up to be counted, you go beyond a personal or private action. Accountability demonstrates your attitudes and beliefs translated into conviction. It embodies *The ABC Formula.* As Scottish philosopher and author, Thomas Carlyle, said, "Conviction is worthless unless it is converted into conduct."[2]

Accountability defines an individual's inherent responsibility for actions, decisions, ethics, policies, and the associated consequences. This responsibility occurs with your willingness to account for what you do, for what you don't do, for what you refuse to do, and for what you don't refuse to do. People read your character in these actions as you demonstrate *The ABC Formula.*

When people lack accountability, they make excuses and blame others. Quick to complain or slow to act, they use phases like: I didn't know; I wasn't there; I don't have time; it's not my job; nobody told me; no one will know; or I just followed orders. Unchecked, a lack of accountability spreads like wildfire in all types of organizations from corporations to communities to churches. That's tragic. Instead, heed this advice from Abraham Lincoln, "You cannot escape the responsibility of tomorrow by evading it today."[3]

With accountability, your actions follow your words. As with initiative, take responsibility today – not some undefined point in the future. With responsibility seized today, you demonstrate accountability. This adds a depth of understanding to who we should strive to be. When you personally demonstrate accountability and responsibility, you earn the right to hold others accountable. So let me ask you this. In what ways are you accountable? Who... or what are you accountable to? For example, are you accountable to your spouse or significant other? Your family members? Your boss? Are you accountable to earn a living? Pay your bills on time? Live up to your word? There may be dozens, hundreds, or even thousands of different ways in which we are accountable.

The brilliant jurist, Daniel Webster, was one of the great thinkers of his time. Once, someone asked him to describe his greatest thought. Before I share Webster's answer, think how you would answer that question. Some might cite a brilliant mathematical equation or quote a wise philosopher. Some might share a significant lesson learned or an "*ah-ha!*" moment.

Without hesitation, Daniel Webster simply answered it was his accountability to God. Think of the significance of his answer. Let that thought linger with you for a moment.

Imagine your arrival at the pearly gates of Heaven. St. Peter asks you to account for your attitudes, beliefs, and convictions. How well do the actions of your life attest for you? Your actions demonstrate your accountability. Ultimately, we are all accountable.

We demonstrate the enduring Core Value of accountability with commitment. It flows naturally from accountability. With commitment, you're accountable. With accountability, you're committed. The two words form a powerful union that Norm lived and taught.

Without them, you're likely to be tossed in the turbulent seas of situational attitudes and beliefs. With them, you're rock solid and enjoy a rich harvest of benefits. Your level of focus increases. You see things more clearly. Your long range vision improves. Your self-confidence improves. Your passion shines through in everything you undertake. Fully brought to light, this enduring Core Value shows the depth of *The ABC Formula*. As your commitment demonstrates accountability, it positively impacts all areas of your life.

Where do we begin on this journey and learn to be accountable to ourselves? Start with commitment to others.

This story provides a beautiful example. One morning, a little girl excitedly got ready to attend her first day of school. She put on her new dress. Her mother bought it specifically for this special day in her life. She kissed her daddy goodbye as he left for work. He told her how proud he was of her and how beautiful she looked. The little girl's face lit up as she anticipated the day ahead.

A couple of hours later, a police car raced up to the school's entrance and screeched to a halt. The little girl's mother bounded out of the police car and rushed into the school room. In a hushed but agitated tone, she frantically spoke with the teacher. Then she grabbed her little girl's hand, and said, "Dear, we have to go. Your father's been in a bad accident."

With sirens blazing, the police car rushed them to the hospital. Time was critical. The doctor met them doctor in the lobby. She quickly explained to the little girl, they needed to take some of her blood to give to her daddy. Only her blood could save his life. After a moment of hesitation, the scared little girl nodded her head in agreement.

After the blood transfusion, the little girl looked up from her hospital bed as her mother came in to comfort her. Mom said, "Daddy's going to be fine. He says he loves you." The little girl smiled weakly. Then Mom noticed a frightened look in her daughter's eyes. She stroked her hair off her brow and said, "What's wrong, dear?"

With tears in her eyes, the little girl asked her, "Mom, when am I going to die?" She loved her dad so much that she willingly made the commitment to sacrifice herself to save him. That's love. It requires faith.

It's unlikely any of us will be asked to commit to something equal to what this little girl thought she did. Take comfort in that. Whatever challenge you face pales in comparison. Fear not accountability and commitment. Avoid being frozen into inaction. Avoid being stuck in a rut. Avoid staying in your comfort zone. Remember, one day you will face the ultimate question of accountability.

To build the enduring Core Value of accountability with commitment, start small. Let it grow as you do. Simply follow through with your commitments. As the famous marketing slogan from Nike says, 'Just do it!' As a visible reminder, I keep one of those Nike pins at my desk. Practice this habit. When you say you'll do something, just do it. Live by this old saying. It's commonly known as 'Grandmother's Rule:' "Do what you say you're going to do, when you say you're going to do it."

It's so simple! Yet, how many people do we know who don't do this? Sadly, it's way too many. Far too many people make commitments in frivolous ways. They say things they either won't do or never intended to do. For the convenience of the moment, they searched for a way to make someone feel good. That approach violates self-control. It violates honesty and transparency. It violates telling the truth. It violates respect. This one example violates multiple enduring Core Values.

Live your life with a simple rule. If something gets in the way of meeting a commitment, let the responsible people know well before the deadline. Let them know well enough in advance, so they can plan accordingly. Then let them know when you *will* meet your commitment.

A noted author and Hall of Fame Professional Speaker, Dr. Terry Paulson promotes 'The Rule of 4' which applies well here. Give an early-warning notice of at least four times the length of the rescheduled commitment. For example, one hour late requires at least four hours' warning. One day late requires at least four days' notice. One week late requires at least a month's notice. Those guidelines help others move resources to cope with missed commitments. They complement the intent of this enduring Core Value.

Consistent actions like these develop your reputation of reliability. People know they can count on you. We *knew* we could count on Norm. I hope you know people like that as well. What a wonderful reputation! It gives people a sense of comfort, stability, and calmness even when times are tough. John F. Kennedy's father understood this well. He said, "When the going gets tough, the tough get going."[4]

The loss of Norm was tough on me and so many others – particularly his family. We were shaken and confronted by the loss of someone who meant so much. He lived his life in ways that left a void in our heart when he was gone. He is sorely missed today by those close to him. But in tough times, you can pull back or *push forward.*

Norm's death began my new journey. I made a choice that night. As I better understood my purpose, a greater focus provided clarity. It led me on a search for greater significance. It can do exactly the same for you. In his book on leadership, John Wooden quoted Dr. Anonymous: "There is a choice you have to make, in everything you do. So keep in mind that in the end, the choice you make makes you."[5]

My search for ways to positively impact people's lives continues today. It's my mission. When you take seriously the challenge to build your enduring Core Values, you fulfill *The ABC Formula* in your life. This deep-seated desire fulfills something meaningfully significant in all our lives.

My journey parallels what's best described in this poem written by Dale Wimbrow © 1934 and first published in American Magazine. The author's son graciously gave me permission to reprint it here.[6]

The Guy in the Glass

When you get what you want in your struggle for self
And the world makes you King for a day,
Just go to a mirror and look at yourself
And see what that guy has to say.

For it isn't your Father, or Mother, or Wife
Whose judgment upon you must pass,
The feller whose verdict counts most in your life
Is the guy staring back from the glass.

He's the feller to please, never mind all the rest,
For he's with you clear up to the end,
And you've passed your most dangerous, difficult test
If the guy in the glass is your friend.
You may be like Jack Horner and 'chisel' a plum,
And think you're a wonderful guy,
But the man in the glass says you're only a bum
If you can't look him straight in the eye.

You can fool the whole world down the pathway of years,
And get pats on the back as you pass,
But your final reward will be heartaches and tears
If you've cheated the guy in the glass.

Accountability with commitment starts and ends with you. Be assured bumps happen along the way. They always do. But with focus and reinforcement, you stay on the right path. Norm understood it, taught it, and role-modeled it to those of us privileged to have quality time with him. I encourage you to build this enduring Core Value in your life and role-model it for others. It will serve you well.

Be Accountable to Your Commitments.

Norman H. Cole

Chapter Eleven Endnotes – Accountability

1. Denis Waitley. BrainyQuote.com, Xplore Inc, 2011. http://www.brainyquote.com/quotes/quotes/d/deniswaitl146947.html, accessed January 5, 2011.
2. Thomas Carlyle. BrainyQuote.com, Xplore Inc, 2011. http://www.brainyquote.com/quotes/quotes/t/thomascarl163811.html, accessed January 5, 2011
3. Abraham Lincoln. BrainyQuote.com, Xplore Inc, 2011. http://www.brainyquote.com/quotes/quotes/a/abrahamlin101733.html, accessed April 20, 2011.
4. Joseph P. Kennedy. BrainyQuote.com, Xplore Inc, 2011. http://www.brainyquote.com/quotes/quotes/j/josephpke141789.html, accessed April 27, 2011.
5. John Wooden, *Wooden on Leadership* (New York: McGraw-Hill, 2007), 43.
6. © 1934 Dale Wimbrow, www.theguyintheglass.com, permission granted by the author's son and accessed June 29, 2011.

PART THREE
NEW BEGINNINGS

The Journey After

A Growing Passion

The Rest of the Story

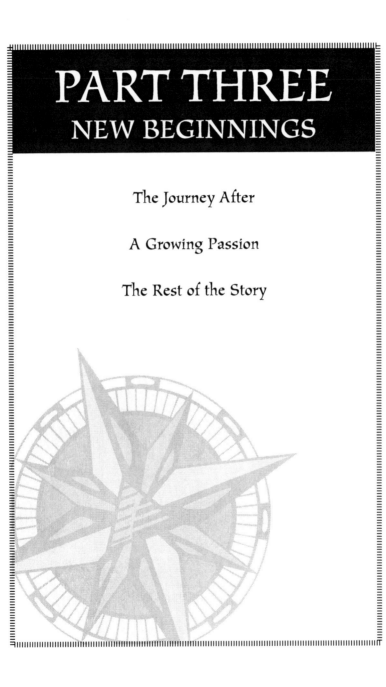

The Journey After

A man may die, nations may rise and fall,
but an idea lives on.[1]
John F. Kennedy, U.S. President

The tragedy of losing Norm described in chapter one started me on a new journey. Immediately, that event impacted me in ways I did not imagine at the time. The loss of someone I cared about so deeply caused me to search for a greater depth of purpose and meaning. Soon afterwards, people noticed positive changes in me. My purposeful focus increased dramatically. My actions better matched my Core Values.

As with any change, obstacles littered the path. But with focus, determination, perseverance, and reinforcement, the direction remains constant. Ever since that painful day, I have kept this reminder with me as my compass.

Personal Mission of William E. Cole (1948 -)
"To positively impact people's lives"

Core Values of Norman H. Cole (1938-1994)
Founder, Advanced Business Concepts, Inc.

1. *Be Respectful of Everyone You Come In Contact With.*
2. *Be in Control of Yourself and Maintain Your Integrity.*
3. *Be Willing to Serve Others and Be There for the Right Reason.*
4. *Be Totally Honest and Transparent.*
5. *Be Willing to Do the Work Necessary to Find Out the Truth.*
6. *Take the Initiative.*
7. *Be Accountable to Your Commitments.*

With this focus and daily reinforcement, I now direct my energy in more meaningful ways. As my self-awareness increased dramatically, the clarity of my mission and enduring Core Values strengthened. As Walt Disney's business partner and brother, Roy, said, "When your values are clear to you, making decisions becomes easier."[2] I attest to that truth.

After Norm's death, I felt unprepared to fulfill what he began. That responsibility weighed heavily on me. I felt our videos needed an update. In my opinion, they were near the end of their strategic life cycle.

For several months, I worked diligently on a business plan. It outlined a strategy to attract investment capital and produce new videos. At the same time, I realized something even more important. I decided to work as hard on me as anything I'd ever done. An uncertain future loomed. I understood the importance of preparing for what lay ahead.

Fortunately, I owned a great asset. Norm developed a series of audiotapes to support our salespeople. The tapes provided a deep understanding of our sales process. But as important, Norm taught us many life lessons.

In the first tape *Benchmark One: Grounding Yourself,*

Norm taught an important process. His words follow with slight modifications made to broaden their applicability. It's my privilege to share these with you.

Benchmark One is to simply ground yourself. However, it begins long before your first interaction, and it is far from simple. During the course of our day-to-day lives there are many factors which can come between us and the achievement of our goals: things like attitude, mood, how we feel physically and personally or family issues, are just a few. In order for us to be effective in our work, see opportunities, relate well to others and have fun in the process, it is vital to address these issues before we get started each and every day. Here are a few ideas for grounding yourself at the beginning of each day.

Take time each morning before starting work and deal with any issues that could cloud your focus. If it is not possible to effectively deal with any given issue, mentally put it aside until another time. If it is an issue that relates to your position at work, discuss it with the person you report to. Things like financial pressure can certainly cloud your focus, and if you are not able to set the pressure aside while you're interacting with others, your financial condition will usually worsen. So if you're dealing with issues that you're having trouble setting aside, ask for help now. Don't wait. Next, give some thought to your purpose in life, that statement which you would like to be remembered for when you are gone. Is it really worth pursuing? If it is, then go after it. If it is not that important to you, spend time immediately and develop a purpose that is worthy of your best effort.

You all know what Thomas Edison is remembered for: the electric light bulb. But the question is, was the electric light bulb a goal for Mr. Edison, or was it his purpose in life? It had to be a goal. If it were his purpose, he would not have continued to invent many other significant items that positively impact the lives of everyone. So what was Mr. Edison's purpose? His purpose was to improve the lives of people. The light bulb was a goal. The storage battery that he also invented was another goal, and the achievement of each of those goals helped him to attain his purpose.

What is your purpose? A definite purpose is a strategic idea, belief or concept that becomes a reflection of your values.

Today, these words ring as true for me as when Norm first recorded them. So let me challenge you. Remember when I earlier asked you to write or refine your Personal Mission on page 30 in chapter two? That's your Purpose. Take a moment right now to re-consider it. Ask yourself these questions. Why were you put here on earth? What are you striving to attain? What are you trying to accomplish? Who do you want to be? How do you want to be remembered?

Your answers define and clarify your Purpose, which I call your Personal Mission statement. You know mine: "To positively impact people's lives." It's short, simple, and easy to remember. It connects emotionally with me and others. Succinctly, it communicates what drives me. Review and re-consider yours. If it's right, affirm it, and write it here again. If changes should be made, make them now in a revised statement.

My Personal Mission is:

_____

_____

_____

Consistently review and reinforce this mission statement. It anchors you. When questions arise, when adversity tests you, or when doubts and fears confront you, it gives you focus. Norm stressed the importance of reviewing it daily and beginning your day well-grounded. He believed this is fundamental to your success. It should be done before you start your tasks each day.

At first, it took practice and repetition for me to make it a habit. As my comfort level increased, it paid large dividends.

Here's what happened. The very day I finished the business plan, a promotional brochure from an international training company landed on my desk. As I read it, amazing parallels to my business plan emerged. Remarkable similarities existed in our two concepts. The company's flagship management training program featured several colleagues of mine from the International Federation of Professional Speakers, as it is known today. I thought that they have already done something similar to what my business plan proposes. Does it make sense to compete with them, or is there a way to collaborate? The intensity of my focus on the business plan caused me to ignore other opportunities. But this brochure outlined a compelling story. I thought a conversation to find out more would be worthwhile.

After some preliminary phone discussions, Ron Cole and I traveled to meet the company's founder, Hal Krause. As we began, Hal set the tone. He said, "What you guys have done intrigues me. It's similar to our concept. I'll be open with you, so you can judge where I'm coming from. Be as open with me as you feel comfortable."

After exchanging a few war stories about our experiences and backgrounds, I shared with Hal this story of how we developed our first video. Our two and a half hour marketing workshop got the company off to a great start. But as with any seminar marketed primarily by telemarketing, the ongoing issue of people who register and don't show up diminished the potential results.

After our first year, Norm devised a way to reach those who missed the seminar and improve our results. He decided to videotape our introductory seminar. Then the video could be delivered to those who missed the seminar. In the classic tradition of entrepreneurial inspiration and spirit, Norm, Ron and I did not let something as small as the lack of video production knowledge and experience get in the way. Excitedly, we followed the advice of Albert Einstein. He said, "Imagination is more important than knowledge."[3]

We bought a camera to record the seminar live. At the time, the longest videotape we found to record and duplicate videos was ninety minutes. I figured out how to cut down the content without diminishing the message. The seminar needed to fit the length of the tape. Centered on the back wall of the seminar room, Ron mounted the camera up high – about 30 feet from the front where I spoke. Finally, it was show time. Ron turned on the camera, and we all hoped everything worked.

As always, I wrote my name on the big white board at the

front of the room. The seminar room's bright white walls, illuminated with bright florescent lights, completely washed out anything I wrote on the videotape. We also had never rehearsed with the camera. As I moved around the stage in my energetic style, I moved in and out of the camera's static picture frame. One thing I know to be true. This was no professionally-produced videotape. But undeterred by such details, we forged ahead.

After the seminar, Ron duplicated six videotapes. It took all night – the best available technology at the time. The next morning, our marketing director delivered the videos to business owners who registered but missed the seminar. His script was pretty simple. He said something like, "We're sorry you missed the seminar last night. Bill was really great, so we brought the seminar to you. If you'll commit to watch it tonight, the only string attached is that I need the tape back tomorrow morning. I need to loan it to others who missed the seminar. Do I have your commitment to watch it tonight and get it back first thing tomorrow?"

As we tracked the results, the numbers fascinated us. We produced more Clients with the videotapes than with a live seminar! How could such a video possibly produce a better result? We later learned that, because of the poor production quality, some people simply shut their eyes and listened to the message. Heard in the privacy of their home without distraction, it produced powerful results.

Inspired by this innovation, Norm, Ron, and I enrolled in professional video training courses. Within thirteen months, we converted twenty two-hour live seminars into twenty hours of pretty good quality video for the time. We supported the video instruction with phone and fax consultation to help business owners implement the systems. That's how Norm franchised Advanced Business Concepts, Inc.

Hal Krause loved our story. He easily related his own

experiences to ours. He asked me how we sold our product. I role-played with him – he bought and I sold. When finished, Hal bowed his head down into his hands. He shook his head to the left and right a few times. He paused for a moment. Then he said, "I didn't think anyone else in the world thought the same way we do. Let's do a deal." That's how I became Crestcom International's first franchisee in the state of California. The other ABC franchisees also joined the organization.

Let's examine what happened and learn from it. I prepared. A window of opportunity appeared. Had I not taken the initiative and done the work before that window opened, I would not have been prepared to take advantage of the opportunity when presented. And opportunities *will* ultimately appear. In a scene in the movie *The Sound of Music*, a memorable line occurs when Mother Superior kicks Maria out of the convent and assigns her to be the governess for Captain Von Trapp and his children. She says, "Whenever the Lord closes a door, he opens a window somewhere." That was true for Maria. It was true for me. It can also be true for you.

The daily focus on my Personal Mission and enduring Core Values provided a consistent reinforcement of *why* I did *what* I did. Ground yourself daily first thing.

Then take on this challenge. Have you established and written your enduring Core Values yet? If not, why not? It's very important to do. The opportunity exists right now. Commit them to writing. Feel free to copy, use mine as a model, or modify the list.

Personal Mission of William E. Cole (1948 -)
Founder, Advanced Business Solutions, Inc.
"To positively impact people's lives."

Core Values of Norman H. Cole (1938-1994)
Founder, Advanced Business Concepts, Inc.

1. *Be Respectful of Everyone You Come In Contact With.*
2. *Be in Control of Yourself and Maintain Your Integrity.*
3. *Be Willing to Serve Others and Be There for the Right Reason.*
4. *Be Totally Honest and Transparent.*
5. *Be Willing to Do the Work Necessary to Find Out the Truth.*
6. *Take the Initiative.*
7. *Be Accountable to Your Commitments.*

Now, it's your turn. Less than three enduring Core Values is too little. More than ten is too many.

My Core Values are:

1. _____

2. _____

3. _____

4. _____

5. _____

6. _____

7. _____

8. _____

9. _____

10. _____

With your Personal Mission and enduring Core Values written, you travel a more focused path. It takes emotional courage and the strength of character to do what most people are unwilling to do. With this established foundation, these significant building blocks guide your more purposeful journey. Congratulations on taking that step! It prepares you for what's next.

Let's return to more of Norm's teaching as you consider your work or career aspirations.

> How does your purpose relate to your organization's mission statement? Define the connection for yourself. That's important to do. It gives you the framework for your values and your goals.

If you're a stay-at-home parent, the same principles apply. This also applies to any volunteer activities you pursue. Make a personal connection between your personal mission statement and the mission of the organization. Do you even know what it is? The more you connect in a meaningful and personal way, the greater your fulfillment will be.

For me, it was easy. My Personal Mission merged with the mission of my new company, Advanced Business Solutions, Inc. As your own boss, they are often one and the same. As Norm continued teaching, he illustrated the connection between the framework of mission, values, and goals in this way:

> Goals are something you strive to achieve over a period of time. Goals without a purpose are not a reflection of your values. Your goal achievement should become the structure for the fulfillment of your purpose. Most people will not commit to a detailed daily goal. The reason is simple, it

is measurable. With a clearly defined purpose and achievable goals, you will have desire, enthusiasm, and persistence. All are needed to be professional.

Remember that fifty-five percent of what you communicate to others is communicated by who you are. And who you are is determined to a great extent by your purpose. So if you have not spent time determining your purpose, I would suggest that you stop what you're doing long enough to consider your purpose in life. This purpose, once developed, will be your source of continual motivation. Remember that motivation comes from within you and without a purpose you will have little or no motivation in the face of adversity.

Now review your personal goals. Your personal goals are a great source of motivation. After all, that's why you're performing the work in the first place, isn't it?

Let's pause and reflect on what Norm just said. He asked us a key question about the relationship between personal goals and motivation. Goals sharpen and enhance your focus. With them, clarity increases. Without them, we move from place to place by accident or chance. While most of us have goals, most of us do not effectively apply ourselves to our goals. Many people get distracted and diverted off their path too easily because of a lack of focus.

Here's my goals' story. I vividly remember one night in 1988, when I watched a Zig Ziglar videotape. He conducted a goals seminar. It was one of those *"ah-ha!"* experiences... a real turning point for me. Early in his presentation, he said simply, "There are two types of people in this world: wandering generalists or meaningful specifics."[4] That got my full attention.

He then suggested this question, "What do I want to be, do, and have?" He recommended writing the answers in three categories labeled: BE – DO – HAVE. Here's what I wrote.

BE	DO	HAVE
Respected	Enjoy life	Money
Loved	Fun things	A nice car
Admired	Professional work	Balance
Comfortable		
Independent		
Healthy		
Happy		

This deeply personal exercise does not need to be complicated. Start small. Keep it simple, but think big. Done well, the words and phrases evoke emotional responses in you. Avoid judgments about what you write as you start. It provides a framework for the pursuit of your goals. Over time, it grows and changes as you do.

So let's get started. Whether you focus on one section at a time or move between sections using free association, it really doesn't matter. Add more sections with words besides 'Be' or 'Do' or 'Have' if you like. These labels simply act as catalysts and springboards. We all approach things a little differently. Avoid limits on your thinking with imposed rigid or inflexible structures. This creates focus for what you want. Do what works for you, but do something, and do it now.

I WANT TO BE:

_____

_____

_____

_____

I WANT TO DO:

_____

_____

_____

_____

I WANT TO HAVE:

_____

_____

_____

_____

If you need additional pages or longer lines, great! Use this format as a stimulus. This exercise might take a few minutes, or it could take much longer. Whatever time you invest will pay huge dividends in the future. Make it relevant for you. That's the key.

As Zig continued, he said that the next question to ask and answer is, 'Why?' I once heard that why is the most asked question and is also the one answered the least. I recommend for each item you write, ask a 'why' question. Many people miss this step. Your answers to the 'why' questions provide you with insight to truly determine the personal relevance of each item.

My questions were: *Why* do I want to be respected? *Why* do I want to be admired? *Why* do I want to be healthy? *Why* do I want to do fun things? *Why* do I want to do professional work? *Why* do I want to have money? *Why* do I want to have balance in my life?

Thank you Zig for what you did for me that evening. You truly opened my eyes to new possibilities. Thank you for what you've done for me and many others. The ongoing impact of your teaching and inspiration in so many areas is remarkable. It's provided me with direction and guidance. I know it's done the same with so many others.

As with anything, it takes time for any process to lock in to where you *own* it. As I kept at it, I refined my list. These phrases emerged:

✓ Be healthy with high energy
✓ Be respected and admired for living a positive life
✓ Achieve financial independence
✓ Take the time to travel and play
✓ Enjoy a comfortable lifestyle
✓ Live a balanced life
✓ Continue growing

Each phrase resonated with a depth of personal meaning. Since I first wrote this list many years ago, only one word has changed. The third item – achieve financial independence is now maintain financial independence. Unfortunately, many people lack self-discipline to apply this. That's why they habitually fall off good resolutions. Answer the *why* questions. Avoid a stall. Build a positively-motivated focus.

In the movie *The Bucket List,* featuring actors Jack Nicholson and Morgan Freeman, the concept is the same. What do you want to do and experience in your life before you die? Ask yourself questions such as these. Who do I want to meet? Who do I want to improve my relationship with? What do I want to learn? How do I want to be remembered? What would I want people say about me at my funeral? I call the last question your C.O.D. – your check out date!

I encourage you to start on this very personal exercise. Review it when you ground yourself daily first thing each morning. Not a static process or a single shot exercise, this dynamic ongoing process turns positive intentions into daily habits. One Client uses this in what she calls her daily "hour of power." Another Client shared with me how he often falters during the day if he misses his morning Bible study. As you gain comfort with the process, you also gain clarity of direction. This framework establishes a focus on your personal goals. It provides a motivational framework for you to continue on a meaningful path based on the *why* you do what you do. Modify and add to them as you grow and change. These broad strategic goals define your vision of the future you. It is written, "Without vision, the people perish."[5] With vision, hope exists. Hope focuses your energy and unleashes a power from deep inside of you. The respected author Dr. John C. Maxwell says, "Where there is hope in the future, there is power in the present."[6]

Next, write out a goal statement in at least one area. As an example, for my strategic goal Be Healthy with High Energy, I wrote down a weight goal. I actually wrote three weights – a short term target, an intermediate target, and a desired target. As Zig says, "How can you hit a target you do not even have?"[7] Turn broad strategic goals into manageable chunks. It's how you change from a "wandering generalist" to a "meaningful specific."

Then apply the SMART goal formula to give you the greatest likelihood to achieve your goal. The SMART goal acronym stands for:

✓ S = Specific
✓ M = Measurable
✓ A = Achievable
✓ R = Relevant
✓ T = Time-Focused

[8]

SMART goals define more tangible targets and therefore more reachable ones. When most people write goals, they are either too broad or include multiple goals. You avoid these common errors when you work on each goal until each one meets the SMART criteria. The following questions help you stay on track. Is my goal *specific* enough and defined in precise terms? Can it be *measured*? Is my goal *achieveable*? Is this goal personally *relevant* for me? In other words, is it really my goal? Am I willing to commit enough focused *time* daily or weekly over a defined time period to do the work necessary to reach the goal?

When your answers are all an emphatic yes, it's a SMART goal. If you decide it's worth pursuing now, then answer these additional questions. What type of *measurement* system will I use to track my progress, and how can I keep it *visible*? What *information* and *resources* do I need in order to accomplish the goal? What *support* do I need as I strive to reach the goal?

A well-written SMART goal begins an important process. But to write and set goals is not enough. Lots of people set goals. Unfortunately, too many do not reach their goals. Some become over-motivated and attempt to work on too many simultaneously. That's called goal diffusion. Ziglar recommends we work on no more than four at any one time. Since our aim should be to reach our goals, we need to shift from goal setter to goal getter. Prioritize your list. Select no more than four SMART goals to work on now. It's fine to start with as few as one. Build the necessary and required habits. That's how you apply self-discipline and focus. As Hall of Fame Professional speaker Jim Rohn said: "Discipline is the bridge between goals and accomplishment."[9]

Returning to Norm's guidance, we see how our purpose and goals are fundamental related our attitudes, beliefs, and convictions in *The ABC Formula*.

Your purpose and goals serve as the framework for your values. With those in place, you can continually increase your effectiveness and consequently your results with the following simple process. Each morning, list ten ways to improve your results today. Spend a few minutes looking at the list you've developed. There might be things like shine your shoes, wash your car, better understand the logic behind some task you perform at work, to improve your sales presentation or handle an objection, or your willingness to hold yourself accountable to a commitment.

You will probably find one or two items that you could do with very little additional effort. The items on your list that will take longer, but would positively impact your results, should be scheduled for implementation in the order of their importance to you. This is a hard exercise, spending time thinking about how to improve, but it is well worth all of the effort you put into it. Try it tomorrow morning, and the day after, and the day after that, until it becomes a habit. Then see the results for yourself.

Your attitude, belief, level of energy, enthusiasm, appearance and other similar factors send messages to everyone you come in contact with. These factors are all a critical part of your success. To have the proper impact on the people you interact with, all of these messages must be apparent to others. Spend time to assess the status of these factors prior to beginning every day.

There is one primary question that I would ask you to consider each morning and again before each and every interaction and that is, "Am I prepared to hold myself accountable for what I've committed to do?" This simple question has a very deep-reaching effect on everything that you do.

You see, I believe that if you are unwilling to hold yourself accountable, then there is no way that you will hold others accountable for other commitments. Commitments begin and end with you, not with others. It is self-discipline and your commitment to yourself and your process that will produce the results, not what others do or say.

Let me repeat that. It is very important to your success. It is your willingness to hold yourself accountable that will, in the end, allow you to hold others accountable for what they want. If you are not prepared to hold yourself accountable, you will not hold others accountable.

Now on the positive side, if you do hold yourself accountable for what you've committed to do, you will hold others accountable for what they've committed to you, but it begins with you. You must be the leader, not the follower. Do you get a sense how important this is? Let me go even further. If you are not willing to hold yourself accountable, you will limit your success. Everything that you do and say – your words, your dress, your comportment and your beliefs, in other words, who you are – begins here.

Norm's words positively impact me. I hope they do the same for you. They contain much wisdom. Write a list of ten things you can do today to improve your results. Work on a few of them. The effect is profound and simple. You consistently find ways to get better at what you do – every single day. I sincerely hope you act on this advice.

As a footnote, I gave Mom a copy of Norm's tapes. She listened to the entire series a few times. Even though she wasn't familiar with the topics, she gained a greater sense of her oldest adult son. Not only was she impressed, she was greatly comforted by the sound of his voice, as I still am today.

As we close this chapter, consider these questions. Will

I summon the emotional courage and instill self-discipline to follow through and hold myself accountable daily? Will I accept this challenge to focus on new habits daily? Am I willing to do the work necessary to condition myself to achieve my goals?

Your answers determine your choices each day. Your opportunity is here right now. Enhance and enrich your life from this day forward. When you do, your passion grows as you do. It's a key building block that we'll explore in the next chapter, "A Growing Passion."

Chapter 12 Endnotes – The Journey After

1. John F. Kennedy. BrainyQuote.com, Xplore Inc, 2011. http://www.brainyquote.com/quotes/quotes/j/johnfkenn125479.html, accessed April 27, 2011.
2. Roy E. Disney. BrainyQuote.com, Xplore Inc, 2011. http://www.brainyquote.com/quotes/quotes/r/royedisne183365.html, accessed April 27, 2011
3. Albert Einstein. BrainyQuote.com, Xplore Inc, 2011. http://www.brainyquote.com/quotes/quotes/a/alberteins129815.html, accessed April 27, 2011.
4. Zig Ziglar, *How to Become a Meaningful Specific* (Krestcom Productions, Inc., 1994 video)
5. Prv 29:18 (KJV)
6. http://www.sparkinsight.com/quotes-by-topic
7. Zig Ziglar, *How to Become a Meaningful Specific* (Krestcom Productions, Inc., 1994 video
8. © Andrejs Zajacs. Professional dart and board on white isolated background ID 18219177. Used by permission from Dreamstime.com for up to 500,000 printed books plus unlimited electronic usage.http://www.dreamstime.com/resolutions.php?w=1987&h=1509, accessed September 22, 2011.
9. Jim Rohn. BrainyQuote.com, Xplore Inc, 2011. http://www.brainyquote.com/quotes/quotes/j/jimrohn109882.html, accessed April 27, 2011.

A Growing Passion

You never achieve real success
unless you like what you are doing.[1]
Dale Carnegie, Author

Purpose lights your direction. Enduring Core Values guide your journey. As you travel your path, well-written SMART goals lay out your plan and measure your progress. This firm foundation drives your actions. As you ground yourself daily, your focus sharpens. Your laser-like concentration helps you prioritize what's important. When applied to the willingness to work on your priorities, your self-control fueled by self-discipline increases your results dramatically. With better results linked to your Purpose, you become successful at something meaningful for you. It's easy then to like what you do.

My wife Kristy swears I've never had a real job. There's much truth in that. I recognize and accept it as a compliment. As my career unfolded, I found joy in my work. I applied my skills and talents to each opportunity. I accepted challenges and grew as a result. Each growth opportunity led to the next one. I've been blessed to live as Harvey Mackay advised, "Find something you love, and you'll never have to work another day."[2] For the vast majority of my career, that's been true.

I also recognize it's not true for everyone. Even though many people work hard and put in long hours, some never find that same joy. And not everyone makes the most of their opportunities or even recognizes the opportunities when they occur. The saying "most people are too busy working to make a living" is painfully true. Let's look at ways to maximize your opportunities, with my experiences as an example.

Initially, I followed the path of music teaching and performance. After my competitive athletic career finished and during my break in college, I coached water polo and swimming. When I re-committed to finish my music education, I studied seriously and taught at the university level. That led to my post-graduate studies which led to instructional development. That led to my overseas opportunity. My growth from that experience led to my first corporate assignment in the training and development world.

In each case, three common building blocks emerged. First, my talent was identified and nurtured. Second, each time I embarked on a chosen path and encountered a fork in the road, I took a risk to try something new. Third, I threw myself on the new path with enthusiasm and worked hard.

Hard work prepares you when doors open. If the work was not done before that door opened, I would not have been prepared to take advantage of the opportunity when it presented itself. If I had not taken a risk, the opportunity would never have been created. Without all those factors in place, I wouldn't have uncovered the opportunities to pour in my passion. Each decision uncovered a new passion.

It was a difficult decision for me to move away from music. I was passionate about my musical career. I invested much in it. In spite of the risk in taking such a big leap into the unknown, I was compelled to move in a different direction. But you never lose that background imprint. All the years of music lessons and performance were not lost. In fact, it's just the opposite. All those experiences contribute deeply to who I am today.

Whether just starting out or in a time of transition, it's often difficult to know what path to follow. It may involve risk. Why do so many people freeze at the thought of risk? There are probably as many answers to that question as there are people. But if you avoid taking risks, not much happens. Things stay the same. Few things change unless you do.

I discovered that risk is part of life. When you walk across the street, it involves risk. When you get out of bed and leave your bedroom, it involves risk. When you stay in bed and hide from your responsibilities, it also involves risk. Remember what Dr. Anonymous said, "Without risk, there is no reward." How very true that is!

Risk creates opportunities. And opportunities exist if you look for them. Right now, you can take a risk to grow within the context of your own job, your classroom, your relationships, or in countless other situations. You could start a business. Those possibilities exist for you right now.

None of us know when our time is up. Norm certainly didn't. But Norm lived his life in a way that reflected his willingness to take the initiative with an occasionally well-thought-out risk. Norm enjoyed a good challenge. He left a lasting legacy and is sorely missed today.

Imagine how you would live your life, if you wanted your legacy to be that people would miss you when you're gone. Imagine how you would live your life, if you wanted people to remember and use the lessons you taught. I strive to do this. It profoundly affects the way you live your life. It's a characteristic of leadership. As the noted author John C. Maxwell said, "Leaders take risks. That's not to say that they are reckless, because good leaders aren't. But they don't always take the safest route. Rarely can a person break ground and play it safe at the same time."[3]

Risk is a choice we make in life. When faced with a risk, we can either be frozen into inactivity, or we can take on the challenge. To assess the challenge and risk, use four questions to analyze the situation.

The first question is, "What's the best that can happen?" Allow yourself to be excited. Your answer creates possibilities and propels you into the future filled with opportunities. Vividly picture what it *could* be. How will it look? Will there be smiles on the faces around you? Will there be a celebration? How is the achievement celebrated? Is there a savory meal involved? Will you take some time off? Graphically *see* the future. It creates energy and excitement.

To balance the excitement, then ask question two, "What's the worst that can happen?" While it's okay to consider it, avoid wallowing in that picture. Guard against the negativity trap where most people freeze up. If they dwell there too much, it stymies them. Remember, there's no reason to wallow in despair. Worst case scenarios rarely occur.

Once you consider the worst case scenario, push yourself to answer the third question, "What's the risk of doing nothing?" Learn from my journey. Attending Syracuse University fueled my decision to switch from music to instructional development. I concluded that, if I didn't take the risk, I would never know if it was the right opportunity. For me, the risk of doing nothing was to look back on a missed opportunity with regret. That's not what I wanted, nor is it what most of us want. Learn from Teddy Roosevelt, our twenty-sixth U.S. President. He said, "In any moment of decision, the best thing you can do is the right thing. The next best thing you can do is the wrong thing. The worst thing you can do is nothing."[4]

We confront many decisions each and every day, if not every hour or even every few minutes. When we're afraid to make decisions, we become immobilized. Encourage yourself and those around us to take a risk. Rarely is too much initiative wrong. Take action. Avoid being frozen in fear. Remember our definition of fear: *false evidence appearing real.*

Take comfort in the fact that none of us will *always* make the right decision. We're not perfect. Not all decisions will turn out to be right. But new decisions can be made to correct previous ones.

The fourth and final question is, "What's likely to happen?" This re-focuses you away from the negative. You already bracketed the best and worst case scenarios. You also considered not acting. Now it's time to consider the odds. Is the upside potential greater than the downside risk? Look at the pros and cons. With better balance in your thinking, you're better equipped to avoid clinging to the status quo or sliding into pessimism. You're more likely to accept or decline the risk based on its merits rather than negative emotions. This process helps you accept risks that are worth taking.

With risk, you accomplish at least two things. First, you start something. At that moment, you don't know how it will turn out. But it just might lead you to do something great. Les Brown, a professional speaker known as the master motivator, says, "You don't have to be great to get started. You have to get started to be great."[5]

Second, as you work through the questions, you realize that the odds are on your side. That breeds enthusiasm for the goal or task at hand. Throw yourself into the new tasks and work with enthusiasm. Dr. Norman Vincent Peale said, "When a person applies enthusiasm to his job, the job will itself become alive with exciting new possibilities."[6] That has certainly been true for me.

Apply enthusiasm to whatever you choose to do, regardless of which path you follow. Learn from Ralph Waldo Emerson. He said, "Nothing great was ever achieved without enthusiasm."[7]

When you move enthusiastically along your chosen path, you unleash your personal power. With focused energy, your success increases. Conrad Hilton, founder of the famous international hotel chain that bears his name, shared this insight: "Success seems to be connected with action. Successful people keep moving. They make mistakes, but they don't quit."[8]

Entrepreneurs and leaders possess a penchant for *initiative*, an appetite for *risk*, an unquenchable *enthusiasm*, and they *persevere*. When I started my corporate career journey, I applied my teaching and instructional development background to a new field and industry. I transferred that knowledge and experience to another industry. I expanded my base of experience and learned the additional human resources functions. Within four years, I was experienced in training, recruiting, finance, and operations in two industries along with direct management experience. I led teams of as many as eleven direct reports.

When Norm's opportunity appeared, I transferred my entire skill set and knowledge base, which led me to professional speaking. I learned new skills in marketing, selling, executive coaching, and consulting. My horizon broadened substantially.

After Norm died, the experience and skills gained led to my affiliation with Crestcom International. I was twice named MVP (most valuable performer) and took on some corporate responsibilities. I was among the top career sales leaders, and my franchise was consistently ranked near the top. I was recognized as one of the top trainers in an organization whose motto was "Trainers to the World." We shared many collaborative successes during our fifteen years together. Thank you, Hal Krause, for the key role you played at an important time in my life. I cherish many good memories.

These same building blocks I used can be just as meaningful for you. I demonstrated a penchant for initiative. I applied myself with a dedicated work ethic. I focused my energy and demonstrated a willingness to stretch and grow. Growth followed. It required ambition and risks. It required focus on where I was going. It also required me to tune out any naysayers. Mark Twain's wise counsel on this resonated with me. He said, "Keep away from people who try to belittle your ambitions. Small people always do that, but the really great ones make you feel that you too, can become great."[9]

Those small people or naysayers may be associates from your past and present. Sometimes, they are inside your own head – when negative self-talk causes doubt and fear. Guard against staying in your comfort zone. It holds you in the drudgery of the present and keeps you ordinary. Tragically, those fears and anxieties trap many people. What a shame! The famous and revered eighteenth-century British preacher, Charles Spurgeon, said it best: "Anxiety does not empty tomorrow of its sorrow, but only empties today of its strength."[10]

Norm taught me a great lesson one day when he asked and answered these insightful questions. He said, "Do you know where good judgment comes from? It comes from experience. Do you know where experience comes from? It comes from bad judgment." How true that is.

As I gained experience, I pushed through mistakes. Fortunately, my foundation was strong. With experience, lessons learned from previous mistakes minimized their impact. More importantly, I avoided repetition of the same ones. My self-confidence grew, and good judgment gained an increasing share.

I learned from my fair share of mistakes and bad judgment. One important lesson I learned early on was to avoid confusing a mistake with a failure. They're not the same thing.

There are only three ways to fail. Number one is to give up. Number two is to announce that you've failed. Number three is to not try in the first place. Push through mistakes and move boldly ahead. Be captivated by what's ahead in the future, and not held back by the past.

My counsel to affiliates is that if they're not making mistakes, they're not trying hard enough. But my other counsel is that when a mistake is made, don't hide it. We can manage anything together but silence. When a mistake occurs, we fix it together and learn from the experience.

If an initiative is taken based on shared enduring Core Values, my affiliates know they'll be supported one hundred percent. If it doesn't work the way we expected, we learn from it. The next actions and decisions will be better. Our culture is built on the encouragement to take action. You can do the same thing.

Encourage yourself and others to step outside of comfort zones. Encourage initiative, risk taking, and performance. Expect them. Based on enduring Core Values, these actions move us most often in the right direction. Make information accessible and freely-shared. Watch the effectiveness of actions and decisions increase.

When that happens, personal responsibility and motivation increases. We accept risk-taking, action, initiative, and mistakes as an investment in growth and forward movement. That inspires us to innovate boldly and pursue new ideas. Excitement builds. Things happen. That's how you encourage a new level of self-motivation that's a model for others to follow. That's when your passion builds and inspires others.

Just what is passion? It means *intense emotion*, and it grows from motivation. Passion is the energy that fuels the soul. This fuel burns on the inside and shows on the outside. The difference between loving what you do and just getting by is passion. It's a natural outgrowth of *The ABC Formula*. People immediately sense passion as it exudes from you. It unleashes your personal power.

Passion leads us to work hard. We vigorously pursue what we love doing. Affiliates with similar passions are drawn into your network. Surrounded with motivated affiliates with similar interests and values, the environment is extraordinary. Everyone is on the same page. The atmosphere encourages visible goals to be seen, shared, and achieved. Innovation flourishes.

With passion in place, then it's a matter of focus. Focus is difficult for many, because they're distracted with clutter in their lives. There's so much going on and so much to do. It's no wonder that it's so easy to get diverted from what's important.

Here's some wise advice from Lin Yutang, a Chinese philosopher: "Besides the noble art of getting things done, there is the noble art of leaving things undone. The wisdom of life lies in the elimination of non-essentials."[11] How true that is! If you invest your productive time in non-essentials, you limit your effectiveness. When you prioritize and focus on what's important more often, your effectiveness increases.

That's why your Mission Statement or Purpose is so important. On this foundation, you build your enduring Core Values. This compass channels your available energy and focuses the pursuit of your passion. Focus enables you to make better decisions and take appropriate risks. As risk inspires action, initiative springs forth. Innovation flourishes. A positive forward-moving culture grows around you. Everyone becomes more successful, whether you lead or are part of a team. Risk-taking creates opportunities to pour out your passion.

In this environment, *The ABC Formula* wells up from inside you and blossoms. Your personal power is unleashed. Your actions better match your words. Your enduring Core Values mold you into a more authentic and congruent person. This combined synergistic foundation makes a decided difference in your life, and you gravitate to things you love. Your life testifies to how you strive to live, so you'll be missed when you're gone. Your life is filled with passion, and significance shines through in all that you do. Then you simply stay grounded. Consistently start your day with Norm's process described in the previous chapter. It's so important. Then learn to re-ground yourself throughout your day and before each important activity.

Here are two ways to do this. Professional speaker and author Jim Cathcart shared this advice with a young entrepreneur who desperately wanted to build his business. You can apply it to any work task or other activity as well. He advised the young entrepreneur to ask this question consistently before any task he was preparing to work on: "How would the person I'd like to be approach what I'm about to do?"[12]

What a *great* question! How would the future me approach the task in front of me now? Consider how significant that is. Before you do something, imagine how the person you *want* to be would approach *this* activity. When you picture the future you doing a task, you will automatically do it with more care, a greater degree of attention, and with higher quality. You will also treat a person you're about to interact with in a more sensitive and caring way. In his teaching, Norm taught us with similar advice.

Do yourself a favor and remember to ground yourself before every interaction. Stop between activities and re-ground yourself. Take time and ground yourself again before entering into a new conversation or activity. Make it a conscious part of your process. Practice it. Improve it with each attempt. You are not wasting time. You are, in fact, increasing your likelihood of a positive result which is the reason for the interaction in the first place. Remember that if you don't take the time to do it right the first time, you will spend more time to straighten it out later, and what a waste. Ground yourself and have the best possible chance at success the first time.

Also, remember that if you're in a long interaction with the same person, re-ground yourself during the interaction. You can do this by simply sitting quietly and taking several deep breaths. Ask yourself a question or two while taking these breaths. Do you understand what the condition of this person really is? Are you really listening and hearing what is being said or are you just listening for an opportunity to speak again? Know your conditions at all times. Knowing your condition will help you maintain the comportment that is required to produce the desired results. It is a continual check. It will become a part of who you are if you will continually monitor yourself.

So let's review ways to keep grounded during the day. When you are starting a new activity, do a couple of things. Try to mentally feel the top of your head or roll the eyes up and look up or physically feel the bottom of your feet. Ball your toes up inside your shoes. Doing things like this will have a tendency to bring you into the present. You might develop any number of things that will work for you. The drill is to simply do something that brings your conscious thoughts together with your body. In other words, be truly present for the interaction and situation.

Now that you're in touch or listening to yourself, take several deep breaths. This will help send extra oxygen to your brain, and with extra oxygen, your brain and consequently you, will be sharper. And you do need to stay sharp at all times. Repeat miniature versions of what you did earlier to start the day off.

Truth rings in Norm's words. Ground yourself daily. Reground yourself throughout the day. Ingrain these habits. Reinforce these building blocks. Follow them with focus and hard work.

When preparation and opportunity combine with passion, talent, skills and the pure love of doing it, it's a joy to see. *The ABC Formula* springs to life. Passion shines from deep inside you. A meaningful, significant life follows.

I'm passionate and excited by what I do. I'm gratified when my Clients' eyes light up when they *"get it"* – when the light bulb goes off inside their mind's eye. We've all had those types of *"ah-ha!"* experiences. I love to draw it out and see it in others.

The key for you is to find something to fulfill your passion. Find something where you can add value to someone's life.

This saying comes from an unexpected source. He was one of the great geniuses of all time. While he had so much brainpower and so many accomplishments to his credit, Albert Einstein also had this wonderful perspective. He said, "Try not to become a success, but rather try to become a man of value."[13]

For me to become a man of value meant to find meaningful opportunities to add value to other people's lives. How do we do that? Take seriously the enduring Core Value of accountability. Use it to de-brief each and every day.

These seven questions guide my review of how well I stayed on track. I offer these as a model for you. Did I...

✓ Start my day grounded with a plan?

✓ Make progress on the priorities I set out to do?

✓ Meet my commitments?

✓ Manage my activities and emotions well?

✓ Let my passion shine through with *The ABC Formula*?

✓ Model my enduring Core Values in ways others could see?

✓ Positively impact people's lives?

When you use these, be honest with yourself. If you don't feel good about your day's activities, commit to improve them tomorrow. With just one improvement tomorrow, and then another the following day, imagine the cumulative effect. One improvement times five days a week times fifty weeks a year is... two hundred and fifty incremental improvements each year. Wow! And that gives you two weeks off from improvements annually. It's not what we know that counts. It's how we use what we know that counts. Commit to get better each and every day. You will live a life of value.

In the dedication and throughout this book, I have credited role models who identified and nurtured my talent. They drew out my potential. They guided the translation of talent into tangible accomplishment. They helped me reach more deeply inside myself and become something more than I was before. As the seventeenth-century philosopher and scientist, Galileo, once said: "We cannot teach people anything. We can only help them discover it within themselves."[14]

Recognition of talent is the first part of the equation. Nurturing and supporting it is the second part. Role models give you perspective and broaden your horizon. They provide encouragement which fuels initiative. Ultimately, they help you realize more of your potential.

People with enduring Core Values become leaders whether or not they have a title. Leadership requires no title or position. Leadership is not something granted by someone else. It is earned through action and character. Leaders come in all shapes and sizes. Others see *The ABC Formula* at work in them. They want to emulate those characteristics. Leaders become role models for others to follow.

Build your enduring Core Values based on what's important to you. Apply your talents, take the initiative, bring focus to what you do, work hard, and persevere. As you gain the ability to take appropriate risks and make better decisions, let your passion shine through in all that you do. While success is not guaranteed overnight, it happens as your passion emerges. It transforms who you are regardless of your chosen field of endeavor. As civil rights activist Rev. Dr. Martin Luther King, Jr. said,

If a man is called to be a street sweeper, he should sweep streets even as Michelangelo painted, or Beethoven composed music or Shakespeare wrote poetry. He should sweep streets so well that all the ghosts of heaven and earth will pause to say, 'Here lived a great street sweeper who did his job well.'[15]

I wish for you to experience this passion. It leads to a new found joy too few experience as they travel on their paths. And here's one final piece of advice from a business icon. Walt Disney said, "They way to get started is to quit talking and start doing."[16]

May your journey be special and meaningful indeed!

Chapter 13 Endnotes – A Growing Passion

1. Dale Carnegie, http://quotationsbook.com/ quote/12451/#axzz1M6CtoKjs, accessed May 3, 2011.
2. Harvey Mackay, Philosophernotes.com, 2011. http://www. philosophersnotes.com/quotes/by_teacher/HarveyMackay, accessed May 3, 2011.
3. John C. Maxwell, *The Right to Lead* (Naperville, IL: Simple Truths, 2009), 69.
4. Theodore Roosevelt. BrainyQuote.com, Xplore Inc, 2011. http://www.brainyquote.com/quotes/quotes/t/ theodorero403358.html, accessed May 3, 2011.
5. http://www.inspirationalspark.com/taking-action-mottos. html, accessed May 8, 2011
6. http://beinspiredonline.com/blog/enthusiasm-quotes/
7. Ralph Waldo Emerson. BrainyQuote.com, Xplore Inc, 2011. http://www.brainyquote.com/quotes/quotes/r/ ralphwaldo101478.html, accessed May 3, 2011.
8. Conrad Hilton. BrainyQuote.com, Xplore Inc, 2011. http:// www.brainyquote.com/quotes/quotes/c/conradhilt130635. html, accessed May 3, 2011.
9. Mark Twain, Quotationsbook.com, 2011. http:// quotationsbook.com/quote/2127/#axzz1M6CtoKjs, accessed May 3, 2011.
10. Charles Spurgeon. BrainyQuote.com, Xplore Inc, 2011. http://www.brainyquote.com/quotes/quotes/c/ charlesspu155631.html, accessed May 3, 2011.
11. Lin Yutang. BrainyQuote.com, Xplore Inc, 2011. http:// www.brainyquote.com/quotes/quotes/l/linyutang107810. html, accessed May 3, 2011.
12. *Managing the Velocity Factor* (Krestcom Productions, Inc., 2003 dvd)
13. Albert Einstein. BrainyQuote.com, Xplore Inc, 2011. http:// www.brainyquote.com/quotes/quotes/a/alberteins131187. html, accessed May 8, 2011.
14. Galileo Galilei. BrainyQuote.com, Xplore Inc, 2011. http:// www.brainyquote.com/quotes/quotes/g/galileogal381318. html, accessed May 3, 2011.

15. Rev. Dr. Martin Luther King, Jr., Think Exist.com, 2011. 15 http://thinkexist.com/quotation/if_a_man_is_called_to_ be_a_street_sweeper-he/339724.html, accessed May 3, 2011.
16. Walt Disney. BrainyQuote.com, Xplore Inc, 2011. http:// www.brainyquote.com/quotes/quotes/w/waltdisney131640. html, accessed May 3, 2011.

The Rest of the Story

Believe in yourself! Have faith in your abilities!
Without a humble but reasonable confidence in
your own powers you cannot be successful or happy.[1]
Dr. Norman Vincent Peale, Author

This chapter title requires a disclaimer. One never knows how much of the rest of the story remains to be written. But I want to bring you up-to-date on what else has transpired in the lives of some mentioned in my journey.

A few years ago, my high school band director, Allan Trefry, and his wife, Mary Ellen, hosted me for dinner at their home. We stay in touch and visited for an afternoon at our house not too long ago. Allan keeps active. He recently competed in the Senior Olympics and won the javelin throw in his age group.

My Syracuse University mentor, Dr. Paul Eickmann, and his wife, Anne, met Kristy and me recently in Sonoma, California. We caught up on each other's lives. Paul retired a few years ago from his position as Vice President of Academic Affairs at the Cleveland Institute of Art. I shared with him how much he influenced my career. We thoroughly enjoyed our time together and look forward to additional opportunities.

Norm's son – my nephew, Ron Cole – owns a video production company, Digital Media. We recently worked together on a project. With two children both grown and married, he's excited to be a grandpa for the first time!

My brother's best friend, Mel Topping and I have become close in recent years. I remember him well growing up. Mom would shush him while I practiced my instruments. Mel also swam and played water polo at Whittier High School. In fact, it was Mel who introduced Norm to his future wife, Kathy, in high school. Mel had known her since elementary school.

After Mel's wife passed away more than a decade ago, my sister-in-law, Kathy, and Mel married. They're happy together, and the family is happy for them. A few weeks ago, Kristy and I enjoyed a nice wine country getaway with them.

Six months after I started Advanced Business Solutions, my wife, Kristy, left her corporate career and joined as our company's CFO. Her administrative and logistical support enriches our lives together. She makes the behind the scenes stuff happen smoothly. It's a blessing to work together. Not all spouses can make that claim.

As for me, I started swim workouts again last year. My high school relay buddies in Southern California contacted me to swim in a reunion relay race. Last year in a masters meet, they swam without me and won first place in our age group. I'm not sure if that's good or bad news! In a recent masters swim meet in Northern California, I placed first in the two events I entered in my age group. I occasionally pick up my trumpet to practice, but haven't kept it up. My goal is to play consistently again at some point. I last performed at a church conference a few years ago.

Speaking of church, a couple of years ago Kristy and I helped start a new one. Epiclesis: An Ancient-Future Faith Community is a small pre-denominational church. The experience enriched our lives and deepened our spiritual growth. It's been one of the most rewarding experiences of our life. We serve and minister to our community and beyond. We post lessons and other resources on our website at www. epiclesis.org. Our most recent analysis shows followers from throughout the U.S. and in fourteen countries. That's led us to form the Ancient-Future Faith Network as a separate entity. I'm on the board of directors, and we already have members across the U.S., Canada, and Europe. We're excited to see where God leads us.

By the way, eleven months after we started prayer and healing gatherings, we called our church pastor, Dr. Chris Alford, my close friend mentioned in the dedication. Dr. Ellen Koehler, my dear friend and primary reader for this book, directs music and liturgy. I occasionally get polite inquires about my willingness to play trumpet in church. But that will need to wait until I retire. And retirement doesn't appear to be anywhere on my near-term horizon.

I recently launched my new course: *The ABC Formula of Leadership*™. Drawn from my expertise, experience, and research, the positive response gratifies me. I accept more speaking engagements now. I continue to coach executives and business owners as time permits. Additional books are on tap. I love to work and learn alongside my Clients. That's my bottom line. As long as my impact is positive on people's lives, my present path beckons. I enjoy work and still have time for fun. No need to retire with *The ABC Formula* at work.

I'm blessed with good health, a comfortable financial position, great relationships, and meaningful work. Enduring Core Values guide my path. A meaningful Purpose drives me each day. That recipe is a result of *The ABC Formula*. I wish the same for you.

These final thoughts sum up my journey well. As Dr.

Norman Vincent Peale said:

> One of the greatest moments in anybody's developing experience is when he no longer tries to hide from himself but determines to get acquainted with himself as he really is.[2]

Thank you for accompanying me on my journey to positively impact people's lives. I wish you well as you travel along your path. Fill your days with meaning and Purpose.

Chapter 14 Endnotes – The Rest of the Story

1. Norman Vincent Peale. BrainyQuote.com, Xplore Inc, 2011. http://www.brainyquote.com/quotes/quotes/n/ normanvinc132560.html, accessed May 12, 2011.
2. Norman Vincent Peale. BrainyQuote.com, Xplore Inc, 2011. http://www.brainyquote.com/quotes/quotes/n/ normanvinc159739.html, accessed May 12, 2011.

About the Author

B ill Cole is an internationally-respected professional speaker, trainer, executive coach, facilitator, and consultant. He was an athlete, coach, professional musician and taught at two universities before starting his business career. Bill's mission is to positively impact people's lives.

Bill's work career includes an international consulting assignment with a Radio and TV network, a national restaurant chain, a fast growth high technology company, and a national business development firm. He served as the 1990-2 President of the Sacramento Chapter of the National Speakers Association and was named the Chapter Member of the Year in 1992. Bill was among the all time sales leaders for an international training company as well one of its top-rated facilitators. In 1996, he founded Advanced Business Solutions, Inc. based in Sacramento, California and serves as President and CEO.

His company provides services in leadership, management, organization, communication, teamwork, entrepreneurship, negotiating, sales, and executive coaching. His first highly-anticipated book is: The *ABC Formula: Building Your Life's Enduring Core Values.*

Bill serves as a church elder and has chaired several boards of non-profit and community service organizations. He enjoys all styles of music, staying in shape, and travel with his wife, Kristy. They were married in 1973. Contact information:

916.853.8562 - www.absinc.org